Mastering Life's
ENERGIES

Also by Maria Nemeth

The Energy of Money:
A Spiritual Guide to Financial and Personal Fulfillment

Mastering Life's
ENERGIES

*Simple Steps to a Luminous Life
at Work and Play*

Maria Nemeth, PhD

NEW WORLD LIBRARY
NOVATO, CALIFORNIA

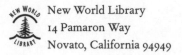 New World Library
14 Pamaron Way
Novato, California 94949

Edited by Yvette Bozzini
Text design and typography by Tona Pearce Myers

Library of Congress Cataloging-in-Publication Data
Nemeth, Maria.
Mastering life's energies : simple steps to a luminous life at work and play / Maria Nemeth.
     p.   cm.
Includes bibliographical references and index.
ISBN 978-1-57731-531-5 (pbk. : alk. paper)
1. Self-actualization (Psychology) I. Title.
BF637.S4N453 2007
158.1—dc22   2006038279

First printing, March 2007
ISBN-10: 1-57731-531-6
ISBN-13: 978-1-57731-531-5
Printed in the United States on acid-free, partially recycled paper

g New World Library is a proud member of the Green Press Initiative.

Distributed by Publishers Group West

10   9   8   7   6   5   4   3   2   1

Dedicated to Aunt Gloria, Uncle Arnold, and my sister, Lisa.

Contents

Introduction

What is the question to which your life is the answer?

I don't believe people are looking for the meaning of life as much as they are looking for the experience of being alive.

— Joseph Campbell

We all yearn to take ideas that excite us and accomplish them through action. We know, on some level, that the ideas we find the most exhilarating are an essential part of us; in a very real way, they *are* us.

The ideas, dreams, and goals that inspire us speak clearly of the contributions we are here to make — that only *we* can make. Tuning in to them, we experience clarity and energy. Listening to them, we see inside us that which is already whole and complete, just waiting to be expressed.

Many times we lose sight of our goals and dreams. Or we spend years analyzing why things didn't turn out as planned or why our vision seems obscured. Some of us discovered that success isn't all it's cracked up to be. We may have accomplished plenty, but we're too exhausted or distracted to enjoy our lives.

I have experienced each of these things. I have also worked for more than twenty-five years with thousands of other people who have had similar experiences — leaders, teachers, ministers, entrepreneurs, physicians, coaches, therapists, students, moms, dads, and friends. Every one of them wanted to know: What is the question to which my life is the answer?

Our lives are shaped by the questions that interest us. In this book we will explore these questions and ease our way into some answers. You will hear voices of those who have already begun applying the principles you are about to discover. But what you will mainly learn to hear is your own clear, brilliant, wise voice. As you do, you will connect — or reconnect — with the energy to live the life you were meant to live. You will gain the tools to bring the energies of money, time, physical vitality, creativity, enjoyment, and relationship to bear on what you truly want. You will learn to create miracles every day, at work and play.

Willa Cather, in her novel *Death Comes for the Archbishop*, speaks to this: "Miracles . . . rest not so much upon faces or voices or healing power coming suddenly near to us from afar off, but upon our perceptions being made finer, so that for a moment our eyes can see and our ears can hear what is there about us always."[1]

As you discover these methods and tools, you will learn to achieve clarity, strengthen focus, enjoy ease, and cultivate grace. You need only bring with you a desire to identify and attain your dreams and goals — along with pen, paper, and a few three-by-five cards!

If you receive catalogs in the mail, as I do, you may have seen an advertisement for an unusual wake-up system. It's a globe sitting on a pedestal, and rather than giving forth an irritating buzz or the sound of music, it wakes you up with light. This light begins dim and then increases until it approximates the brightness — the luminosity — of sunlight. It is my hope that what you read here does the same for you. May you awaken to luminosity by mastering life's energies, and may your eyes see and your ears hear what has been around you — and within you — always.

STEP ONE

~~~⁓

Achieving Clarity

CHAPTER ONE

Being Luminous

*Are you willing to live your life
with clarity, focus, ease, and grace?*

*Twenty years from now you will be more disappointed by the
things you didn't do than by the ones you did do.*

— Mark Twain

The *Encarta Dictionary* defines *luminous* as "emitting or re-flecting light, startlingly bright, inspiring, radiant, resplendent, stunning, splendid."

Our experience is luminous not when we are *thinking* about living our lives, but when we are *fully engaged physically in reality*. The experiences that reflect luminosity are those based on actions taken with clarity, focus, ease, and grace. By *clarity*, I mean seeing what is truly important and creating a game worth playing and goals worth playing for. By *focus*, I mean directing our energies and attention toward accomplishing what calls to our hearts. By *ease*, I mean venturing farther than we normally would in going for our dreams — with a bit of elegance instead of struggle. Finally, *grace* means being consistently grateful and using spiritual principles so that we are ever aware that all is well.

Luminosity — it's worth emphasizing — is clarity, focus, ease, and grace *in action*. It can't be invoked by psychological insight or analysis. It's fresh. Luminosity doesn't comb its hair but rather lets the winds of life blow freely through it.

My friend Aimee had a luminosity wake-up call while sitting over cappuccino and croissants with orange marmalade on her fortieth birthday.

"I was in a local coffeehouse, sitting alone at my favorite table, reading one of those books that help you take stock of your life. One question stuck out: 'What do you want people to remember you for?' Suddenly it dawned on me that I didn't know what people would say about me. And then I saw something I didn't like. Given what I focused on when I talk to my friends, they'd probably put the following on my tombstone: 'Here lies Aimee. She had issues.' That definitely wasn't what I wanted to be there. I wanted something more."

Luminosity is about that "something more." It is about taking a deep breath and knowing that all is well. It is about being successful without being exhausted. It is about locating your natural heart of compassion and seeing what you really want to be doing with your life — not what you should do, not even what you ought to do, but what you really *want* to do.

I know about the "issues" Aimee referred to. As a clinical psychologist, I've been trained in different psychotherapy approaches. I was in psychoanalysis myself as part of my training — three times a week for ten years. Lying on a couch, I talked (and talked) about my issues. To be fair, much of what

I discovered helped me become less anxious and more centered. But my problems and dilemmas consumed my attention. They took center stage when I talked with friends about what I wanted to do with my life. It never occurred to me that continually analyzing my problems was not the key.

Then, as I approached my own fortieth birthday, I got restless. I was bored with how I thought and talked about my life. In the early eighties I went to a series of seminars on self-transformation. A light suddenly turned on. I glimpsed a new way of thinking that wasn't based on diagnosing and treating what was wrong. In those seminars we looked not so much at why we thought the way we did but at what we were doing with our lives. I saw that everyone wants to know that his or her life makes a difference — that we all count for something.

Still, I didn't attain luminosity. I took what I learned and single-mindedly pursued my goals and dreams. But it went too far. After a while I saw that I had become, as my friend Ellie put it, a "success object." I was a walking, talking success machine. I was doing a lot — driven to raise the bar, go farther and faster, to prove myself. I compared myself with every other person who was successful and always came out on the bottom. You've probably never done this yourself ... or have you?

As a result of all this activity, I achieved goals but was often too exhausted to enjoy what I had done. I looked for what was next, never what was right in front of me. It was no fun.

We really do teach what we need to learn. For example, I wrote *The Energy of Money* to help people use money in accord with spiritual principles so that they can be prosperous from the inside out.[1] The book came about because of a bad business investment I had made, and so I spent years teaching these

principles to others so that they wouldn't make similar mistakes in their own lives.

Now I'm learning about luminosity, even as I write this
book. Luminosity is about living the life you were meant to
live, without running yourself into the ground and driving
those around you crazy. I have been privileged to learn about
luminosity in the presence of about fifty thousand others —
ministers, millionaires, mentors, students, health-care profes-
sionals, grandparents, in short, people of all ages and interests
— who have taken seminars from me over the past twenty
years. What you will find here is their stories, along with the
principles that emerged for living the luminous life.

The luminous life isn't predictable. It isn't tied up in a neat
package. In the now-famous series of interviews Bill Moyers
conducted with Joseph Campbell about the hero's journey,
Campbell talked about how unpredictable life is and how difficult it is to see what may happen in the future.[2] In fact, life is
confusing, and things don't always make sense. Campbell told
a story about King Arthur's knights searching for the Holy
Grail, which was hidden in the middle of a dark forest. Each
knight had to enter the forest in the darkest place for him,
where there was no path. The reason for this was simple,
Campbell said, because if you could actually see a path in front
of you, it wasn't your path but that of someone who had gone
before you.

Later in that interview series Campbell talked about what
happens when we look back on our life. That's where we begin
to see how everything fits, and we make sense of the decisions
we made.[3] We say to ourselves, "Oh, that's why it was important to move to Seattle," or, "Now I see how lucky I was to

meet Tom just when I did." Looking back, we get a sense of continuity.

Imagine you're stopping for a moment and turning around to look back on your own hero's path. You see that all along it are strung beautiful round paper lanterns, the kind that people hang on trees during the summer. Each one casts a golden glow that illuminates a part of your trail. As you continue to look back, you see that whether the sky was a royal blue or gray and overcast, these lanterns shone nevertheless. Sometimes fog settled in, but you could still see the warm light from each globe. Now consider that each lantern represents a luminous moment that you designed and put in place. Wouldn't that be great to look back on? You could see without a doubt that indeed yours was a good life.

The Call to Luminosity

You deserve to live the life you were meant to live, and you have the energy to do it. It's time to focus that energy instead of wasting it. And by energy I mean your money, time, physical vitality, creativity, enjoyment, and relationships. All these are forms of energy that you and I can learn to focus toward what we truly want in life. We can master this energy or remain frustrated and in a perpetual bad mood.

Luminosity summons images of light and radiance. All of us want moments in which there's enough light that we can see clearly all the possibilities open before us. We want our eyes to see and our ears to hear what has always been there.

Luminosity is also about going toward the light, being in love with the light and not even worrying about getting away from the darkness. I've learned that whatever I try to get away from only follows me, nipping at my heels. Going toward the light gives more hope. It takes less energy than trying to get away from something — and it's much more fun.

There, I've said it. *Fun*: the *f*-word. A friend once told me something like this: "I want to get enlightenment, but I don't want to be so heavy about it. This enlightenment stuff sounds so serious. Can't I just have a little fun?" (The answer is yes.)

It takes guts to turn your attention away from what you think is wrong with you, others, or your work environment — to turn from complaints to contribution. It takes daring to become focused on dreams instead of dilemmas. You could get worried that if you don't look at your shortcomings — or those of others — something bad will happen. You may be so used to looking at your problems and concerns that the thought of leaving them behind sends chills through you. Later on we'll see why this is so and give you a way to go beyond your worries as you travel on the road to luminosity.

But right now, just to begin, ask yourself, "Would it be all right with me if life got easier? More fun?" We might get suspicious of a question like that, wondering, "What's the catch?" or "How does this apply to my work?" Get used to it. I'm going to ask you that same question a few times in this book.

The Difference between Happy Moments and Luminous Moments

Luminous moments are different from happy moments. Yes, luminosity includes happiness. But as we define them here, luminous moments involve focused action.

Happy times look like this: I was eight, and my mom owned a bakery. On this particular day the bakers had made a three-foot tub full of dark bittersweet chocolate icing. They used about ten pounds of pure sweet butter and real vanilla. You could smell it all through the bakery. The trouble was, this batch was overcooked and too dark to use. There it sat on the kitchen floor, a tub of lukewarm dark chocolate icing with just the slightest pool of melted butter on top. It called to me as I stood over it. I looked up. Mom was watching, a smile twinkling in her eyes. As though she had read my mind, she said four words: "Go ahead, do it!" And I did. I plunged my arm down into the warm, dark, sweet chocolate. The icing oozed between my fingers. I drew my arm out of the soft icing and started to lick it off. My arm smelled like butter for two days.

But a luminous moment looks more like this: I was twelve. I had worked at the bakery and saved up $20. I caught the bus and went to a department store to buy my mom a Mother's Day gift. I saw a gold-plated pin in the shape of a sheaf of wheat. It was $19.95. I plunked the money down, bought it, and gave it to my mom the next day. I was nervous because it was the first time I had ever gone out on my own to buy her something. What if she didn't like it? She opened the package, looked at the pin, and burst into a big smile. She told me it was perfect and how creative it was of me to give her something that reminded her of baking. My heart soared! I felt so proud.

It's now almost half a century later, and my mom has long since passed away. Burglars broke into my home many years ago and took almost everything my mother left me, all the great rings and jewelry she had bought over the years. All, that is, except for that gold-plated pin shaped like a sheaf of wheat. It's been with me through ups and downs over the years, and it always reminds me *how* I made my mom happy that day.

The difference between a happy moment and a luminous moment is this: in luminous moments *you have taken action* on something important to you. In the happy moment, I enjoyed that luscious warm fudge icing all over my arm. I was in the right place at the right time and knew from my mom's look and encouragement that she loved me. But in the luminous moment, I knew that my mom knew that I loved *her*. I had taken focused action to show my mom how precious she was to me. Luminous moments occur when you generate something important from inside yourself and make it real in the physical world. Bringing it to pass takes energy that you have to focus. It might even involve risk because you might fail.

Think about times in your past that were great, that you'd characterize as "the best." Where were you? What were you doing? And that is the key question: What were you *doing*?

Were you writing a book, mentoring a colleague, composing a song, taking your kids on a white-water-rafting adventure, planting a garden, talking with a patient or client, cooking dinner for friends, or comforting a family member? Was it a moment when you finally picked up the phone and called a friend just to say you love and appreciate them?

As a result of taking that action, you may have experienced a quality that people associate with a luminous moment. Whatever you were doing, look at the quality of that instant. Perhaps you experienced elements of quality that look like this:

- You see possibilities that are open to you. You see the *yes* in life rather than the *no*.

- You see promise in situations or circumstances that seemed doubtful.

- You see the answer to a problem that had seemed to be unsolvable.

- You know you have whatever it takes to meet the challenge or adventure that is before you.

- You are centered, even in the swirl of activity and change.

- You see the obstacle before you as an opportunity to develop new skills.

- You recognize that you are doing what you are meant to be doing — right here, right now.

- You are grateful to be alive — that you are living *your* life and no one else's.

- You appreciate and delight in the moment — the color of a flower, the sound of someone's laughter, the smell of wet grass.

- You have compassion for others, your generous nature is awakened, and you want only the best for them.

- You know that all is well.

I was elated when I saw my mom's smile as I gave her that gold-plated pin. I felt so proud that I had met the challenge of getting her that piece of jewelry. I had saved up the money and, for the first time, taken a bus alone. This was big.

Now I wear that pin whenever I have a challenging meeting to attend or a talk to give for which I lack a bit of confidence. It reminds me of the time when I chose a goal, worked for it, took a risk — and it worked.

It's Not How Much You Do but What You Do

I was once driven to do many things in life. People who love me have told me that sometimes all the activity made them dizzy. I'm naturally active, but the driven quality came about because I failed to make an important distinction: the busy life isn't the same as the successful life. Lots of activity does not equal accomplishment. It is possible to do "big" things but be so exhausted, cranky, and depleted afterward that you feel emptier than when you started.

I ask you to entertain a different definition of success: *Success is consistently doing what you said you would do with clarity, focus, ease, and grace.* Success, seen this way, is an inside job. You don't compare yourself to anyone else. You don't even look at whether what you're doing is big or small. You look instead at the *quality* of your action and of your experience. Success is not about dragging yourself across the finish line or up the mountain.

Speaking of mountains, let me illustrate what I mean. About two years ago I hiked to the bottom of the Grand Canyon with seven girlfriends. It was June and hot — 118 degrees at Phantom Ranch, at the bottom of the canyon. As you hike down the canyon, you're literally going back in time, reading Mother Earth's autobiography. You pass pink layers of rock, then red, then heavy, dark, old, old, old rock that's been there for a billion years and looks like it's been burned in a million fires. The bottom is like a convection oven; you feel the heat radiating off the rocks long after the sun sinks behind the canyon walls. The coolest it gets at night during the summer is around 90 degrees.

My goal was to hike down the Grand Canyon, and back up,

with dignity. I wasn't going to crawl or claw my way to the surface as I'd done three years before when I'd pushed myself to climb up as quickly as possible.

This time, halfway down the Kaibab Trail, I realized that my hiking boots were too old and weren't supporting my feet. Hence my toes banged against the boot casings with every step. Any hiker will tell you that one mile like that is painful. Eight miles downhill were excruciating! At the bottom, when I took off my boots, I saw through the blisters that I would lose four toenails.

So how did I snatch clarity, focus, ease, and grace from that situation?

The hike back up took me fourteen hours. Normal hiking, pushing myself a little, would have allowed me to finish in eight. Two of my friends bounded up the trail to finish in five. The rest of us decided not to push ourselves and stopped frequently. We carried water pistols, and when people passed us, we squirted them. Then we'd talk with them and laugh. This was a good thing because the heat in the canyon soon rose to over 100, and everyone needed to be cooled down. This also took my mind off my feet! And every time we stopped, it gave us a chance to *really* look at the rocks.

Pain is pain, no matter how you look at it, but this time my experience wasn't one big complaint. I forgot about comparing myself to the hikers who'd made it to the top faster. I took the trail literally one step at a time. I got to the top of the canyon with dignity and smiling — despite the fact I was minus four toenails.

In the busy and driven life, there's no clarity, focus, ease, or grace because there's no room for them in the flurry of activity.

Moments of elation are followed by longer periods of exhaustion. I call it *busyholism*, and we look at it here because the minute we talk about taking action in life, some of us start to hyperventilate, thinking it means we need to get even busier. We worry that our daily to-do list will only get longer. But the truth is this: clarity, focus, ease, and grace are principles that *decrease* the amount of our activity because what we're doing becomes purposeful and focused.

So, if you are going for luminosity, you may have to lower the bar. That's right, I said lower the bar, not raise it. We've learned to raise the bar on our hopes and dreams to a sometimes impossible level. This keeps us either driven and revved up, on the one hand, or lethargic and resigned, on the other.

Instead, you're going to look at what sings to your heart. You will create something we'll call a game worth playing, and you'll choose the goals worth playing for. You'll learn how to gather and focus your energy — your time, money, physical vitality, creativity, enjoyment, and relationships — so that you get what you really want. You'll also learn how to go past that point where you've given up on yourself. You will go from busyholism to accomplishing what is dear to you. But the price you may have to pay for all of this is lowering the bar — going for less, not more.

Let me tell you a success story about someone we'll call Sally. She was twenty-eight when she first came to a seminar I led on how to become financially successful. Tall, with a big smile, she had just gotten off welfare and had a job cleaning homes.

Sally wanted to be financially successful. The definition of financial success is doing what you said you would do with money — with clarity, focus, ease, and grace. The amount of money is not important. I know millionaires who are not financially successful by this criterion; instead, they are worried about money, afraid that they'll lose what they have, convinced that people like them only because they are rich.

Being financially successful was a big challenge for Sally. As she put it, "No one in my family has ever even talked about being financially successful. I want to know that I'm doing something with my money instead of just having a one-night stand with it."

Sally set a goal: an investment portfolio with $600 in it by the end of one year. This would demonstrate her intention to be financially successful.

Every month Sally would work extra hours to put $50 in an investment portfolio savings account. That may not be a huge amount of money, and for Sally it was a bit of a stretch but by no means impossible. By our definition of success, each time she regularly deposited a $50 check, she was demonstrating financial success.

At the end of one year she had $600. She put it in that investment portfolio. "I'm going to put $100 a month away now!" she said.

And so she did. I happened to see her a few months after she put that $1200 into her investment portfolio. She looked like a different woman. Her clothes were more professional, and she was putting herself through school, but what I remember most is what she said about the process: "I thought you had to have confidence and feel better about yourself *before* you could be financially successful. I waited a long time for that to happen. Now I see I had it backwards. When I got that first $600 and did

what I said I'd do, I automatically felt better about myself —
like I could take on the world!"

How much — quantity — is not what's most important
here. Conventional wisdom tells us that you have to save up
larger amounts of money in order for your investments to
count. But is that really true? In a spiritual or metaphysical
sense, amounts are simply inconsequential. It's the quality of
the action — in this case action taken with clarity, focus, ease,
and grace — that determines your experience of luminosity.
And luminous experiences encourage us to persevere, to keep
going. It's the consistency that pays off in the long run.

Success and Luminosity: Just a Matter of Skills

You have everything you need to function perfectly on your
hero's journey. Nothing has been left out. There is nothing
wrong with you, and there never has been. I say this no matter
what you have experienced in your life.

Please let that sink in for a minute. Getting just this from the
book might allow your heart to relax and your stomach to calm.
Do you realize how much energy we spend with our heart tense
and our stomach all tied up in knots? That's because we are worried that at the center of everything, something is wrong with us.

Whatever you have gone through in life or are yet to go
through, your experiences are the natural consequences of
being a human being. You are already on the hero's journey. It
always looks like this. And on this journey, you already have
several things going for you: a good heart, the capacity to
dream, and the desire to make a difference. How do I know?
It's true about everyone, whether they know it or not.

What also may be true about you, as for many of us, is that you have not yet developed the skills you need to attain the goals and dreams most important to you. That's all that's necessary — learning a few skills.

What this means is that you don't need to change who you are and even what you think. There's no need for a makeover. The only thing you need to do is learn to bring forth what is already within you so that you dance with life in the way you were meant to dance.

To illustrate, let's imagine that you buy a new car. It's fully loaded with extras. There's only one catch: you've never learned to drive. Now let's say that you get into this car as soon as you buy it, start it up, and drive away with it. Would that be a logical thing to do? No, you'd quickly get into some sort of trouble, maybe even an accident.

Now let's suppose that after your accident you begin questioning what's wrong with you that you didn't know how to drive. You start to analyze your faults and shortcomings. Maybe you get the "insight" that you have driving "issues" or that your lack of ability is related to an urge to "self-sabotage." You might wonder if you have a fear of successful driving and your fear led to your accident. Given all those other folks driving merrily along, something must be terribly wrong with you.

The truth is that nothing is wrong with you. You simply haven't learned the skill of driving. Once you do learn it, you're off and running, visiting places you've always dreamed of. And amazingly, at the very moment you do this, all your self-analysis drops by the wayside. Your attention is no longer focused on the internal "stuff" because you are having too much *fun*.

The first skill we're going to learn is how to separate your doubts and worries about what you can or can't do from something much more powerful inside you: your capacity for *being willing*.

Nevertheless, I Am Willing

People who are successful are willing to do what they don't want to do. They are willing to do what they are afraid of doing. They are also willing to do what they don't know how to do. They have learned to say yes to their lives. Swedish diplomat Dag Hammarskjöld captured this well. He said, "For everything that has been, I say thank you, and to all that will be, I say yes."

Say yes to all that will be, and you're taking a step every bit as courageous as those knights who entered the dark forest in search of the Holy Grail. Think about it. You put one foot in front of you. You don't know what your path will look like, but you are going ahead anyway. No more standing at the outskirts, waiting for the trail to show up. You have begun. Even if those customary, limiting inner thoughts are yelling at you to stop, you're on your way.

Say yes to all that will be, and you're giving life permission to serve up your experiences fresh from the oven. No cooling necessary, no added ingredients. You will take what you are given and will appreciate what is offered. You will take it in, digest it, and use it to wake yourself up to everything around you.

But how do you say yes? One way is to say, "I am willing."

By simply being willing, you automatically energize yourself to take action. This is true no matter how long you've put that action on hold. You get in touch with the power that resides in your hero's heart.

Before we go any further, let's look at the difference between *being willing* and *willingness*. Some words are more powerful than others. Powerful words light up our hearts while other words bring little or no energy with them. The words you use in everyday life will direct your attention. Ultimately, they affect how capable you experience yourself to be. I have worked with thousands of people who liberated themselves from old doubts and worries simply by seeing the difference between *willingness* and *being willing*.

Willingness is a noun, along with words like *eagerness*, *readiness*, *oneness*, and *openness*. A noun refers to a thing, an object, and because it is a noun we experience it as outside ourselves. For example, when we say, "I have willingness," we're treating it like something we possess — like a car, a glass of water, or a cute cat. "I have willingness" says nothing about who we *are*, and that's why it isn't as powerful as "I am willing."

Try this out: say "I have willingness" out loud. Next, say "I am willing." Which statement gives you more of a sense of possibility and promise? Which has more energy attached to it?

"I am willing" is the most potent statement you can ever make. It signifies that right here and right now you are ready to go ahead with your life without being forced. You are voluntarily participating, no longer being dragged onto your life's path leaving heel marks in the dirt.

Here's where the *nevertheless* comes in. *Nevertheless* means "despite a situation or circumstance," "all the same," "even so." To put *nevertheless* in front of *I am willing* means that even with my doubts, fears, judgments, evaluations, attitudes, states of mind, and points of view — even with the usual, limiting internal chatter going on in my head that tells me to turn back, to wait a while, to retreat — I am saying yes to my life's adventure. I am willing.

Right now, please take a piece of paper or a three-by-five card and write "Nevertheless, I am willing" on it. Carry this with you for the next three days. When you hear the usual chatter that comes up every time you contemplate moving forward on an idea, dream, or vision, hold up those four words and read them out loud. Note what happens to your energy.

And that's only the beginning. . . .

CHAPTER TWO

Driving in the Fog

*To have clarity in your life, you must first see
where clarity has been lacking.*

*If we continue down this path, we're liable to end up where
we're headed.*

— Traditional Buddhist saying

There is no way around it: if you want clarity in your life,
you first have to see where, up until now, clarity has been lacking. There's no leapfrogging to lucidity without understanding
where you're leaping *from*.

It's a challenge to become clear — to wake up, become conscious, and stop bumping into life. When we wake up, we see
what is really important and valuable to us. We can see the path
that has been waiting for us all along. We can begin to live the
life we were meant to live.

It's nice to wake up sooner rather than later so that you
don't have to repeat the same lessons over and over (and over)
again. As you've probably noticed, when you are in the "not

that again" pattern, the lessons only get bigger and harder. Life is trying to get our attention, to wake us up. If we're in a deep sleep, this can be a real jolt.

Imagine you're driving on a country road. A gray fog swirls around you. Turning on your headlights only seems to make it worse. Suddenly the fog clears and you see that you're driving on the wrong side of the road — and that a ten-ton truck a quarter of a mile away is coming straight at you.

Do you pause to ponder how you got on the wrong side of the road? Do you think back to your parents' driving behavior and try to figure out how it might have affected your own? Do you work on accessing your "inner driver"?

No! You pull over. You get out of the truck's path. Your actions are clear, focused, and simple. That's because you woke up.

But imagine the thick fog does not clear. It continues to obscure your vision. You don't know you're on the wrong side of the road, and even though you occasionally have to swerve to avoid oncoming traffic, you keep driving along, still in a fog, still on the wrong side of the road. But because of your frequent near misses, you begin an internal dialogue: Why does this keep happening to me? What's my problem? Do I secretly enjoy minor traffic accidents? Why do I attract all these cars? Why do I keep sabotaging my drives? I must be thinking the wrong thoughts; if I thought more positively, maybe this would stop happening to me.

Preoccupied with these thoughts, you find yourself even more prone to the run-ins you are so busy trying to understand.

Many of us have become spiritual roadkill on our hero's path because we're asking the wrong questions. Some, like the ones above, might actually cause the fog to thicken. At the very least, asking those particular questions doesn't lead us to change lanes so we can keep out of harm's way.

I'll give you some specific ways to lift the fog from your path, including better questions to ask. Applying these techniques is exciting because when you lift the fog, when you see clearly where you are, you will intuitively know what to do next.

Let me say this again. It sounds so simple, so obvious, that we might miss it. (We tend to think important truths have to be complex and hard to grasp.) *When you see clearly what is before you, you will know in your heart what to do.* Your actions will be simple and precise, with no wasted effort.

When the fog lifts and you see the truck speeding toward you, you simply move over to the right lane. No one has to tell you to move over, and you don't need any advice about how to do it. You don't need to mull it over; your actions are natural, instinctive, and effective.

This is because you have a wellspring of wisdom within you just waiting to be tapped.

"That may be well and good," you say. "But do I really need the ten-ton truck in my path? I got out of the way, but it was a close call, and I was pretty shaken up." Good point. What we want is gentle course corrections, adjustments made with ease instead of dramatic swerves. We want to see the truck when it's *five* miles away, realize our lane error, and move over without all the heart pounding.

That is our aim here: not just to lift the fog, but also to do it in a peaceful, graceful way. Small adjustments and no big messes to clean up — imagine the energy saved! How creative could we be with such clarity instead of wearing ourselves out coping with one near miss after another?

Your fog may be a vague sense of frustration, resignation, or cynicism when it comes to your important dreams. You are frustrated because you think you don't have the time, money, imagination, or physical vitality to tackle them. You are resigned to putting them off until life settles down and you're under less stress. Or you have cynically given up on even dreaming the dreams that thrill your heart. You are convinced that is for other people, not for you.

If you are in touch with thoughts like these, congratulations! They are part of the fog, and before you can clear that fog away, you have to realize you're driving in it.

The Nature of the Fog

The inner conversations that discourage you from going for your dreams may seem fresh and convincing when they're going around and around in your head. That's the nature of the fog: punch at it, and it absorbs your fist. Wave your arms to brush it away, and it laughs at you. Shine the headlight of analysis on it, and you just get more glare.

Allen, who dreamed of a career selling gemstones, had a fog that went like this: "I want to travel to faraway bazaars looking for amber or hike to remote mountain villages where they sell the best jade. But first I've got to figure out how to get rid of my fear of failure. I have these success issues that have been with me for years. I'm working on dealing with them now. But I'm not ready to make a move yet. When these feelings improve, I can talk to someone about what it takes to get into the gemstone business, but I need to handle all this first."

To see your own fog, try this: Get four pieces of paper. With the first paper in front of you, think of a goal or dream that you've put aside until . . . Now take a deep breath and list all the reasons why you've put it off. Do this quickly, and try to empty out your mind. Even if what you write doesn't make sense, keep writing down all the doubts, worries, and "issues." What are the excuses you've given yourself or others? Get them all down.

Then think of another goal or dream you haven't pursued. On the second piece of paper, write the reasons for this dream deferment. Be as specific as you can.

Finally, think of a third, unrelated goal, preferably one from another area of your life. And you know the drill: get all your reasons down on a third piece of paper.

Now read over what you've written. You'll likely see some words or phrases repeating themselves regardless of the specific dream. You might even spot a theme or story line. (What you lack, how others thwart you, a pattern that goes back to your childhood, or a recurring feeling.) Take that fourth piece of paper. First put an *A*, and write all these recurring themes, words, or phrases down under that heading.

Now we get to the mechanism behind the mist. On that same fourth page, write down a *B*. Then think of everything you have told yourself about *why* these reasons make sense. What do you tell yourself about why you have these particular worries, doubts, frustrations, and issues? Jot these reasons down under *B*.

Look at *A* and *B* on that fourth page. What you now have is an outline of how your mind looks when caught up in self-analysis. You might feel uncomfortable or tense when looking at this. It may feel claustrophobic or sad when you realize you've been living with these thoughts.

Trained as a psychologist, I became adept at analysis. I learned how to hunt down, bag, skin, and truss just about any explanation or rationale. I discovered how to serve them up in a stew — and I've eaten that stew myself, convinced that all these reasons nourished me. They didn't. Taking them in only forestalled the inevitable: seeing that I wasn't moving forward or creating what was important to me.

Here's a personal example: I'm in the psychology department's old building at UCLA, in my dissertation adviser's office. I explain to him why my mother's conflicted relationship with success has made it difficult for me to finish the chapter I had promised to write. I believe what I'm saying, but he just chuckles, "That's a good one! Okay, I'll give you two more weeks." I'm relieved; I got the extension I wanted. But as I leave his office I'm also embarrassed: was that excuse really necessary? It sure didn't leave me with a sense of satisfaction.

Much later I went to a weekend seminar in San Francisco, where we were asked to look at the words we use to describe ourselves. I saw then — as my adviser had seen years before — how much energy I used focusing on my internal conflicts. I remember stepping out of the seminar building and thinking: Did Martin Luther King Jr. have control issues? Did Margaret Mead have family-of-origin conflicts? Did they care if they did? Or were they too busy living out their goals and dreams? What were the questions that guided their lives, and how did they differ from the ones I was asking myself?

Don't misunderstand me, there's a time and place for analyzing doubts and worries and for looking at situations in the past that call out for healing. We all need to make sense of our thoughts and feelings. But there comes a time when we are just spinning the same yarn, again and again, with little to show for it. We remain as we are. This can be true even if our thoughts are deep — *especially* if they are deep.

I'm not suggesting you stop using your analytical powers. I'm asking instead that you consider the ways habitual thought patterns stave off luminosity. We all have these habits of thought, and they are tenacious because they've become routine — habitual. They've become routine because they have an internal logic; they have "worked" for us in a sense, if only to account for why our lives have turned out as they have. But when we bring only these old patterns of thought to life's fresh adventures, we run the risk of turning the new into the old.

It is important to acknowledge that our thoughts are hard to control. For example, if someone mentions hot fudge sundaes and then tells you not to think about them, what do you get? Rows of them dancing in your head! Recognizing this is actually good news. When we realize our thoughts are not going anywhere, no matter how much we poke and prod at them, and when we see that poking and prodding them actually creates more fog, we can relax.

In this relaxed state we can shift our attention away from these repetitive doubts and worries and focus it instead on something that's more interesting to us — our deep-down dreams, for instance.

This is really the fundamental key to luminosity: focus on what you love, what's interesting to you, what sings to your heart. What you focus on creates your experience of reality. If you focus on endlessly processing your issues, doubts, and dilemmas, you get fog. Focus on what you want to create and contribute, and the fog begins to lift. Strengthen this focus muscle (as you'll learn to do in the next section), and the fog recedes further. "Foggy" days or moments will always come around, but they become the exception, not the rule.

A Way Out of the Fog

To paraphrase Albert Einstein, we cannot solve problems with the same level of thinking that generated them. Analyzing issues and dilemmas can get us to one level. But we want to go on to another level, a *luminous* level. One way to achieve this level is by learning to observe.

I learned a lot about observation in a chance encounter with a Magic Eye image, those computer-generated images that initially make no visual sense. The idea is to try to see a three-dimensional object embedded in the seemingly chaotic design.

It was a Saturday morning, and I was at a mall. Magic Eye posters hung everywhere. One poster, about two by three feet, was a jumble of blues, greens, and purples. A sign at the bottom read *Dolphins in the Sea.*

I stepped up, squinted, and then crossed my eyes. No dolphins. I stepped back. Still no dolphins. I really got frustrated when two little boys ran past the picture and yelled, "Hey, look at the dolphins!"

I stuck with it, trying to analyze how to see the dolphins and worrying about why I couldn't. Nothing happened until I relaxed. I stopped struggling, took a deep breath, and let my gaze soften. I stopped trying to force the image and instead let it come to me.

At first, what happened wasn't all that pleasant. I could tell my perceptions were shifting, and this was a bit disorienting. The pattern in front of me was changing, but I didn't yet see the dolphins. I was somewhere in between, and this made me want to look away.

I can think of many times I've "looked away" because a problem or situation wasn't immediately clear. It's uncomfortable to stand still while seeing nothing or being confused. Learning to observe teaches us how to stand still until what wants to show up can emerge.

That morning in the mall, as I stuck with the discomfort at seeing "nothing," an image of dolphins playing in the surf began to emerge. Had they been there all along? Of course. I had just not developed the skill to see them.

The following exercise will help you develop that skill of seeing, one of the many skills we'll discuss that create an opening for luminosity.

Over the next week, notice a time when you need to make a decision but you're stumped. You don't know the answer. It could have something to do with work, home, your health, anything. Instead of frantically asking yourself or other people what you should do, ask yourself the following:

- What is there for me to *see* about this situation that I may not be seeing yet?

- What is important or meaningful to me about this event or circumstance?

These are unusual questions. They ask you to step back from the situation, and answers may not be automatic. Sit tight. Nod at but refuse to engage the voice in your head that insists you must have a solution *now*. You might write the questions on a sheet of paper and jot down whatever responses come to mind. You are orienting your attention in a different direction; you are shifting from asking, "What should I do?" to just observing. Stop writing after about five minutes and put the paper aside.

After some time has passed, even just an hour or two, return to what you wrote. Consciously relax your mind and soften your gaze as you read. Look for the presence of one or more of the following:

- Words or phrases that give you a sense of breathing room or that speak to your heart
- An idea that gives you a sense of promise or possibility
- A changed perception of the dilemma itself
- Anything that prompts the sense that all is well

Observe what emerges from this exercise. I guarantee you'll see something you hadn't seen before. It may be small and subtle or so big and obvious that you have one of those "Who's buried in Grant's tomb?" moments. You'll see these things because you have widened your view. As with the Magic Eye posters, the answer is waiting for you; you just need to develop the skill to see it. And be assured, you have the natural ability to learn this skill; your capability just needs to be fostered.

The basic idea is this: when you learn to observe where you are, when you lift the fog of endless self-analysis, you will intuitively know what to do next.

Let me end this chapter with another illustration of what it's like to observe.

You're swimming in the warm, clear waters of the Caribbean. You come upon a yellow fish, swimming along, humming to himself, minding his own business. He's a talking fish, so you say, "The water's great today, isn't it?" The fish says, "What's water? What are you talking about?"

It doesn't matter what you tell him about water. For the fish, there is no such thing as water. This is because water is all he knows; he's got nothing to contrast it with.

But let's say that at some point, this fish gets very happy and starts jumping. At a moment of intense delight, he jumps so high he gets out of the water. There, for one instant, he observes what he's been swimming in. He now knows what water is — and isn't.

What happened as the fish observed water? First, in jumping above the water, he created an observational gap. In order for you to observe something, you must create or recognize a space between you and what you're observing. In that gap, you realize that you are not what you are observing; it's not you.

Second, what the fish gained in the observational gap was the ability to contrast water with something else — air. And once this distinction's made, it cannot be unlearned. Once the fog lifts from the road you're on, you can't unsee the truck coming toward you.

CHAPTER THREE

A Game Worth Playing

Life is luminous when we create games worth playing
and goals worth playing for.

I fairly sizzle with zeal and enthusiasm as I spring forth with
a mighty faith to do the things that ought to be done by me.

— Charles Fillmore, cofounder of the Unity School
of Christianity, in his nineties

Y ou've probably heard some version of the expression "Life's a game." It's sometimes said with a note of skepticism, as if nothing in life is really worthwhile. But what if we discovered that life really is composed of a series of games, some serious and some fun, and that the well-lived life consists of creating personal games that are worth playing because they involve goals that mean a great deal to us?

Remember Sally, whom we met in chapter 1? On her road to financial success, she set the goal of having an investment portfolio. I met up with Sally about eight years after her first investments.

It was a sunny spring day at a riverfront restaurant in Sacramento, California, and a woman at an outdoor table near mine looked familiar but hard to place. When I heard this woman laugh, I knew it was Sally. How different she looked! Yes, her clothes, hair, and posture had changed, but what struck me most was a quality of calm self-assurance. She had shed pounds, but her face told me she had dropped loads of mental baggage as well.

That day Sally told me, "I'm not the same person I was when we set up that game worth playing. It wasn't really setting aside the money, it was doing something I'd set out to do that was important to me, consistently and without struggle. Each month I put away fifty dollars made me feel better and better about myself, and this sense of succeeding spilled over into other areas of my life. I began to think about careers in a way I never had. People cheered me on, and I let their support in. Today I'm a real estate broker — and I get to mentor other women in how to be successful in their lives. Can you believe it?"

I could believe it, and I loved hearing Sally's story. Stories like hers — of people who come from dire circumstances and go on to develop productive, creative, meaningful lives — give all of us hope. They can also give us a blueprint for our own goal setting and achieving.

From prehistoric times, when people competed at throwing stones, we have been drawn to "the game." Games allow us to clarify our goals, learn new skills, cultivate our talents, and focus our energies. When we see people playing their personal game worth playing — whether that's building a nest egg or a better computer, finding cures for disease or finding time to pursue a creative passion — we feel their sizzle and recognize their zeal and enthusiasm.

Turn to your own life, and think of an unrealized dream. To develop a catering business, write a book of poetry, swim in a Caribbean lagoon, volunteer for the Red Cross — whatever it is, look closely, and you'll see that the goal asks you to stretch, develop skills, and engage with life in new ways.

Engagement — dancing with your dreams — and luminosity go hand in hand. Think about it: haven't you felt best about yourself when you were involved with a project or activity that had significant meaning for you? It could have been as big as starting a community program for at-risk youth or as small as tutoring one child. In reality, none of this is small if it's about expressing yourself and bringing what was inside you out and into the light.

This is what I mean by games worth playing, and this is how important they are. You choose these games, and they reflect who you are in a profound, personal, and meaningful way. They focus your energies and cut your doubts and fears down to size. In a very real way you are shaped by the game, for as you develop needed skills, you come to appreciate your own capacities. You begin to define yourself apart from your old excuses, experiences, and explanations.

This is what Sally did. It's what athletes "in the zone" do as they play with clarity, focus, ease, and grace. And "the zone" is not an extraordinary state to be enjoyed by only a select few. You too can define your game worth playing and play your way to success. Doing so will add purpose and passion — sizzle — to your life.

The Elements of a Game Worth Playing

Psychologists and sociologists have studied games for years, and most agree that they share the following fundamental qualities:

- Structure: a playing field and one or more players
- Goals, and the objective is to win or attain these goals
- Obstacles to attaining these goals
- Skills that must be developed to play the game competently and overcome obstacles
- The possibility of losing or failing to attain the goal due to the obstacles
- Rules of engagement
- Feedback, which lets the player know how well he or she is playing

I wrote that games shape us. In sports, this is obvious; you can often tell what sport an athlete plays by the shape of his or her body. On a more subtle level, you can also observe how people have been shaped by the games — or roles — they've chosen in their personal and professional lives.

We are shaped by the games we choose to play because playing requires clarity. We ask: How is this game structured, and what are the goals? How do I get around obstacles? What are the rules? By being clear about these things, we focus our attention and actions. Some events become more important and others less so; we learn to screen out irrelevant information and ideas. Clarity about where to apply focus — what you find essential — affects both your experience of life and how you show up in life. Clarity shapes you. (This is what struck

me years ago as I considered whether I wanted to be known for
my ideas or for my "issues.")

Why Obstacles Are Important

Obstacles are at the heart of every interesting and worthwhile
game. We recognize this when it comes to sports, but in our
own lives the single most important reason we never begin to
play for what we truly want is fear of the obstacles we know or
suspect we'll encounter.

But what would it be like to play a game without obstacles?
Imagine you're on a soccer team, and before a game your coach
announces that the other team couldn't make it. You're going to
play anyway, but without an opposing team.

Pregame excitement gives way to confusion. On the field,
you have the ball, you run for the goal, and you lob one into
the net — easy with no guard blocking your shot. This happens
again and again.

How long would this game hold your interest? Games
worth playing contain the chance to win, and winning involves
overcoming obstacles. There has to be something to push
against, go through, run around. There also has to be the possibility of losing. When we lose, we are called on to reinvent
our strategy so that we might prevail the next time around.

The opportunity to lose gives games their spice. Have you
heard the one about the gambler who dies and goes to hell? He
finds himself in a room filled with gaming tables — roulette,
blackjack, poker. The dealers stand waiting for him. The gambler thinks he's in heaven until the devil hands him a fistful of
chips and explains that he can't lose, no matter how long or how

much he plays. As the gambler places bets and plays cards, hitting all his numbers and getting twenty-one every time, he realizes he's doomed. With no challenge and no thrills, he knows he is going to "die" of boredom.

We don't want to lose, but we do want a challenge. Winning and scoring are great, but if we dig a little deeper we realize that the thrill is in developing our skills so that we can win despite the obstacles.

This may sound intuitively obvious when we think about driving a ball deep down a fairway or hearing that "pop" when the ball hits the sweet spot on our tennis racquet, but in our everyday lives we often act like we don't know this. No matter what we begin — writing a book, painting a picture, opening a business — we often panic and freeze when we come up against an obstacle. We start talking ourselves out of the game. We decide we don't have the necessary time, money, or talent. We doubt our wisdom and our worth.

Can you imagine a soccer player running with the ball, getting blocked by an opponent, and then stopping on the spot and quitting the field because there wasn't supposed to be any opposition? No, the player knows to expect obstructions. *They're part of the game.*

Obstacles and challenges get us so alarmed about ourselves or our goals because we lack clarity about what the playing field looks like and what the rules of engagement are. What if we saw that what happens when we're challenged is what is *supposed* to happen? What if we saw obstacles as a sign that we're doing something right, not something wrong? With this understanding, wouldn't we be encouraged to keep going? Maybe we'd even enjoy ourselves as we do!

Again, think back to a peak experience in your life. Were you required to learn something new or otherwise stretch beyond your comfort zone? Did you have to anticipate and overcome a hurdle or two? Whether it's learning to ride a bike, speak a new language, or solve crossword puzzles, everything we learn involves meeting a challenge.

Playing toward Luminosity

The feature that most distinguishes a game worth playing is that it is personally meaningful or relevant to us. The game must call out to us and resonate with who we truly are; it must give us an opportunity to express our innermost intentions.

I use the word *intention* in a specific way: intentions are the purposes or aims that lie in our hearts and give us a sense of meaning. In working with thousands of people, I've found that some intentions are universal and important no matter our age, gender, professional status, or spiritual orientation. Because they are usually with us for life, I call them Life's Intentions.

We usually think of intentions in a different way. For example, we might say something like this: "I intend to lose weight"; "I intend to take a vacation"; or "I intend to get a job." These reflect desires. While they may be important, they don't have the depth or significance of a Life's Intention. They can be relatively short-lived. There's no sizzle.

In contrast, Life's Intentions are a way of being. In themselves, they don't point to specific actions or goals. Instead, they exist as possibilities that call out to us in a fundamental way. They can be a source of vitality for us, no matter what is going on in our lives. Here are some examples:

- To be physically fit and healthy
- To be a generous friend
- To be a creator of beauty
- To be an effective mentor ,
- To be financially successful

Many people report that they feel their heart relax when they read a list of Life's Intentions. There's an opening, some breathing room, a sense of spaciousness. This is because Life's Intentions reveal what is right about us rather than what we think is wrong. They indicate our ideals and priorities, not our failings or perceived lacks. Life's Intentions fuel our hero's heart and are the foundation for designing the games that are worth playing for us.

Life's Intentions also contain within them the possibility of contributing to others in some way. You contribute to someone else by doing something for them. You can give them money or mow their lawn. You might show them in many ways how much you love or respect them. Just as powerful, you might give them the gift of letting them know how important their support is. Finally, you just might inspire them to take action in their own lives because they see what you are doing with yours.

While Life's Intentions in and of themselves are not about taking specific actions, they nevertheless pull you toward wanting to achieve something. The root of the word *intention* means "to stretch." Once you discover your Life's Intentions, you'll find that you naturally think about how to realize them.

This is how you create a game worth playing: take a Life's Intention that calls to your hero's heart, and then find a way to demonstrate it in physical reality. In other words, create a goal worth playing for.

The G-Word

Goal is a dirty word for many people. It conjures up boring pushups at 5 A.M. or pushing ourselves to lose weight or pay off credit card debt. That spacious feeling that comes from looking at a Life's Intentions list fades. Let's try to rectify that situation.

Webster's defines a goal as an area or object toward which play is directed in order to score. *Play!* That means goals can be enjoyable. They are also specific and measurable. They have a beginning, middle, and end. You attain them and then go on to the next goal. It's possible — you'll see — to craft goals that warm your heart and nurture your spirit.

But for now, it's enough to see that at the heart of a game worth playing are goals worth playing for because they spring forth from your own Life's Intentions.

This is what such games worth playing can look like:

Life's Intention: To be a successful author
Goal: I write a children's book.

Life's Intention: To be a creator of beauty
Goal: I plant a rose garden.

Life's Intention: To be physically fit and healthy
Goal: I hike 10 miles on the John Muir Trail.

The combinations are endless, the possibilities all around you. You take a Life's Intention that calls to you and develop a goal that is related to it. And voilà! You have generated the basic conditions for luminosity. That's because you are bringing that first luminosity prerequisite — clarity — into play. I can't begin to count the number of people I have worked with over the years who have been frustrated into giving up on themselves simply because they neglected to get clear about the game or games they really wanted to create.

When you engage with your personal games worth playing, you redefine who you are, just as Sally did. You stretch and experience vitality. You sizzle because you are claiming success on your own terms. You are not comparing yourself to anyone else's personal paradigms because you are tuning in to your own inner guidance.

The Playing Field

To succeed at any game, you must clearly see the playing field. This gives you an idea of what to expect. Many of the difficulties that get in the way of pursuing our dreams stem from a lack of this kind of clarity.

I've heard the following from people frustrated by their lack of success:

- Why does it get so hard when I'm going for something I *really* want?

- I do want to reach this goal, but I only have so much energy. How can I do it without wearing myself out?

- How can I tell if I'm on the right track when the going gets tough?

- There always comes a point when it just becomes a chore. Even if I was sure I wanted it, it stops being fun.

That's when I want to stop or switch to another goal, so I wind up with a lot of unfinished projects. Why does this keep happening?

You likely have your own version of the above. If so, you're in good company because the people who asked those questions are capable, intelligent, and creative. But even capable people sometimes don't see the playing field clearly. The bottom line is this: once you know the layout of the field, it's a lot easier to bring clarity, focus, ease, and grace to your game. So here is a brief description of the playing field, focusing on its two main aspects, physical reality and metaphysical reality.

Physical Reality

Imagine reality as a blank canvas in front of you. Now draw an imaginary horizontal line across the middle of the canvas. Below this line is metaphysical reality, and above it is physical reality. Of course, there is no real line. Yet drawing this line helps us clarify that the two domains of reality differ in many important ways. In fact, your own success depends on knowing the difference between them.

Each domain has its own rules. Many people who are creative and bright don't accomplish what they desire because they don't know the rules of each domain.

The revered Buddhist monk Thich Nhat Hanh said, "The miracle is not to walk on water. The miracle is to walk on the green Earth in the present moment."[1] Physical reality is where we "walk on the green Earth." Here the energy is dense and thick. Objects — trees, rocks, water — exist here because they have weight, mass, and size. You can quantify them. They can be seen. Physical reality is tangible, concrete, and measurable.

Physical reality is dense. This means that to move, create, adjust, or modify anything in physical reality takes energy. We're talking here about playing the piano, throwing a pot, driving a car, writing a play, riding on horseback, raising money for your favorite charity, or otherwise interacting with things that can be seen, tasted, touched, smelled, or heard. Physical reality — not only is this where the rubber meets the road, this is where both the rubber and the road truly exist!

In addition to being dense when it comes to energy, a second feature of physical reality is impermanence. Physical reality is always changing. It isn't stable. Whatever is created lasts for a time in its present form and then disappears. Nothing remains forever in only one form.

Whether you know it or not, even your personal experience of reality is constantly changing, moment by moment. The following experiment will illustrate what I mean:

1. Hold your two index fingers up at eye level.

2. First look at your right finger for about five seconds.

3. Now look at your left finger for five seconds.

4. Now direct your attention back to the right index finger.

Do you notice that your right finger looks even the slightest bit different from the first time you saw it a few moments ago? You are probably not aware that the second image of your right finger is showing up differently on your retina than did the first. The image of what you are looking at, and how this affects what is happening in your visual cortex, is constantly changing. Even when staring at a flower or glass of water for a few seconds, your eye is making minute adjustments. The image is continuously being altered.

What keeps us from getting confused is that the brain is what we might call a perceptual averaging device. The second time you look at your right index finger, the brain compares it to similar images from the recent past and finds a match. It says, "Ah! The right index finger! Just where I left it last! Hasn't changed a bit!"

Can you imagine what your experience of life would be like if your brain were incapable of making these instant comparisons in order to maintain a sense of stability and permanence? What if your immediate short-term memory was somehow impaired and you lost the ability to make these perceptual associations? Something similar happens to people with certain types of brain trauma. They become excruciatingly disoriented since everything they see — people they met a few minutes prior or people they've known for a lifetime — they see as if for the first time.

So far, we have two characteristics of physical reality, density and impermanence. The third quality is unpredictability. When we work in physical reality, we're subject to surprises. How many times have you started your day with a to-do list and a schedule, only to have to change things around within the first two hours — or the first fifteen minutes? This is an aspect of life that we all deal with. Somehow, the day usually doesn't go as planned. The pictures we have in our minds about how something is going to turn out usually don't correspond to what actually happens. That's because unpredictability is so — predictable!

If you want to predict something accurately, it's possible. All you have to do is keep your span of time very short. For example, if I want to predict the weather with a fair amount of accuracy, I can do it as long as I forecast what's going to happen in the next few minutes. The problem is, a prediction like this is not very useful or interesting.

It's more interesting to lengthen the time span of the prediction, say to one day. But then accuracy suffers. It gets worse when I go to three days or one week. There's no way around it: unpredictability is a natural feature of physical reality.

Unpredictability is also a built-in obstacle when it comes to playing your game. Beyond a relatively small interval of time, chaos sets in. There's nothing you can do to stop it. You never know exactly how everything is going to turn out. You may have a detailed plan for a taking a vacation in Hawaii, making a garden, remodeling your home, or giving birth to a child. But your mental picture about how you want the future to look rarely corresponds to how it actually shows up in physical reality. How do you deal with unpredictability? *You learn to dance with it.*

Density, impermanence, and unpredictability: these are the features of physical reality. They are also the features of any exciting game. Take golf, for example:

- Density: How will I hit that ball? What iron to use? How to adjust my swing?

- Impermanence: The wind just changed. A cloud passed in front of the sun. A tree is waving its branches in my line of sight.

- Unpredictability: Fill in the blank here! How often do we place a shot exactly where we want it?

All interesting or exciting games have the same three features. Why are these qualities so interesting in a game and yet so infuriating when we experience them day by day? Why do we think that life, as it is presented to us, should be any different?

Physical reality frustrates us. For one thing, many of us believe that if only we plan everything and do the right things in our lives, we'll get exactly what we want when we want it. Sometimes this does happen. But more often, just when we think things are going according to plan and we "have it made," our path takes a turn or twist. Something unexpected happens. Our house doesn't sell when we wanted. That company puts off our consulting contract for three months. When we need to shift our plans to accommodate, we often worry that we have done something wrong to cause things to turn out that way.

But this isn't true! Most of the time we haven't done anything wrong at all. It is simply the nature of physical reality.

We want to become resilient in the face of impermanence, density, and unpredictability — in the face of physical reality. Metaphysical reality is where we can obtain guidelines that show us how to dance with the life swirling around us.

Metaphysical Reality

When you drew that imaginary horizontal line, you placed metaphysical reality below the line and physical reality above it. That's because metaphysical reality is like the ocean and physical reality like the waves that dance on its surface. The waves are impermanent, changing, and have form while the ocean is constant; it doesn't disappear as do the individual waves.

Seeing metaphysical reality as the support or foundation for physical reality gives us a more immediate and intimate view of it. Metaphysical reality isn't somewhere up above, detached from us and only occasionally coming down to pay us a visit. Instead, we emerge from it. We sit on its lap. We are never far away from it.

Metaphysical reality is impossible to map or measure. It isn't quantifiable like physical reality. However, these two domains do share one attribute in common: energy. But the difference is that in metaphysical reality energy is not limited by the density of form and is therefore much higher. Form, you'll recall, belongs to physical reality.

Instead, metaphysical reality is the home of ideas, dreams, and visions. The energy there excites us. Ideas can be electrifying. Who hasn't experienced the thrill of a great thought? In metaphysical reality, anything is possible; there are no limits. We don't have to worry about being realistic or even logical. We can soar with our imagination to any place we want right here and now. Think of the freedom! Fly down to Rio right now in a luxurious jet? No problem. Lift a piano with one finger? Done!

All this excitement can be seductive. We might become so thrilled that we begin to think that having a great idea is the point of it all and so neglect to do anything about it in physical reality. (Like the novel that stays in your head or the business plan that never leaves the planning stage.)

We can also get confused when we treat ideas the same way we treat physical objects. We can come to think that if we get excited enough about our ideas, they will materialize by themselves. That's the fog setting in.

Metaphysical reality is where we find guidelines for bringing certainty to the unpredictability of physical reality. This is where our voice of wisdom lives, along with our Life's Intentions. Later on we'll discover how to tell if we are listening to our voice of wisdom or just driving through more fog. Armed with this knowledge, and in touch with what's important to us in the form of our Life's Intentions, we will be ready for our game.

Metaphysical reality is also the home of timeless spiritual principles that we can use to wake ourselves up, to lift the fog from our path. Our ideas about physical reality are always changing; think of how quantum physics has in some ways supplanted our Newtonian view of the world. However, spiritual principles — what it takes to live fully — virtually never alter or change. The guidelines are as valid now as they were two to five thousand years ago. We look at this more in Step 4, "Cultivating Grace."

Why We Need Both Metaphysical and Physical Reality

It doesn't matter how exciting an idea is. If we stay in metaphysical reality too long without taking action, we're going to "metafizzle." This is not a pretty sight — a lot of gnashing of teeth and wringing of hands. No matter how brilliant or creative our ideas may be, without action we get frustrated, irritated, and difficult to be around.

At the same time, if we just take action in physical reality without relating it to anything substantive in metaphysical reality, we become driven. Our lives lack meaning. We live from one to-do list to the next, ending each day exhausted and unfulfilled. We begin to ask ourselves: is that all there really is to life? Sogyal Rinpoche writes about this in *The Tibetan Book of Living and Dying*.[2] Our activity comes to resemble a swarm of flies buzzing around on a hot summer afternoon: lots of noise and movement but not much direction.

Both of these conditions are extremely uncomfortable. That's where the "game" comes in. Take something important to you in metaphysical reality, marry it with a specific target in physical reality, and you have a game worth playing and a goal worth playing for. Your action is anchored and you are centered. You have found a bridge between the two worlds, clarity about what is important in the game, a way to measure if the goal has been reached, and a sense of fulfillment once the game is complete.

But here's where things get even more interesting. Remember that a game requires a series of obstacles in order to capture our attention and hone our skills. Well, the minute you try to bring an idea into physical reality, you're in for a shock. It's a situation that has always confronted people, no matter how creative or accomplished they may be, which is why it's surprising that we get so shocked. I call it *Trouble at the Border*, and learning to cross this border is another key to luminosity.

CHAPTER FOUR

Trouble at the Border

---

*Realizing your dreams and ideas in the physical world
entails a border crossing.*

*The road to satisfying experiences must necessarily pass
through the terrain of discomfort.*

— Gregory Berns, author of *Satisfaction*

Did you ever find a hot idea suddenly turn cool on you, even
as you tried to put it into action? What was once temptingly
exciting got too hard or too complicated or took much more
time to do than you ever thought it would. Perhaps you were
starting your own coaching business or learning to ballroom
dance or — well, it doesn't much matter what the idea was,
something happened. Something always happens when you start
a game worth playing.

Trouble at the Border is the name I give this fog-generating,
murky place we all go through as we start to play toward a goal.
The good news is that Trouble at the Border is a sign — paradoxically — that you are on the right path. You read that right:

this "trouble" is natural, even good. When I first recognized this, it was as if a lead weight sitting on my heart suddenly turned to feathers and blew away.

I'm going to describe this border experience in detail. You need to be crystal clear about your own version of it, so I'll show you how to observe your experience of Trouble at the Border. Remember, we're not analyzing here, just observing so that we can gain some perspective and cut through the fog to see what to do next.

Real-Life Trouble at the Border

Here's a common, real-life example of Trouble at the Border that I've heard from a number of people: "I want to be physically fit and healthy. It's one of my biggest Life's Intentions. Do you know how many diet books I own? I see one with a catchy new title and snatch it up. Then I start to read it. Then I stop because I'm sure that it won't work for me, and besides I've really read it all before."

It was a hot idea, then it cooled off. Every time you try to bring an idea into physical reality — every time you try something new — you're going to meet up with this internal chatter because you are crossing the border between the high energy of metaphysical reality and the density, impermanence, and unpredictability of physical reality. It happens when you begin any game worth playing. There's no getting around it. No matter how much you analyze it, it won't go away. (Believe me — I've tried!)

I go through this experience every time I start writing a new chapter. Beginning this one brought it on big-time. I spent a day feeling heavy, tired, and sure that I didn't have the energy to write about this. I used to think I was the only one who got the energy sucked out of me or that for sure there was something wrong with me or with the project. This time around, since I've written books before, I thought that surely I'd earned the right to skip this part of the hero's journey. Nope.

All of us have our personal border-crossing experience. Even though we think Trouble at the Border means we should stop in our tracks and back away from the game, it doesn't mean that at all. It really means that we're up to something big and that all is well. I know — try telling yourself this when you're going through it! That's why I'll show you how to develop skills to meet even this part of the journey with luminosity.

Say you have a Life's Intention to be a creator of beauty. No problem there. It's clear and easy to see. So you choose a goal to demonstrate that intention in physical reality: an English garden with a fountain. Still no problem. But then you begin to design and plan the garden. Suddenly you come out of that rarified atmosphere of vision and idea and into the density of physical reality. Questions come up:

- Where will I find someone who can help me design the garden?
- What kinds of plants should I choose? What color? What size?
- Where will I find the time, money, or creative energy to put this all together?
- Should I plant this myself or get professional help?

These are important questions; they help get the project going. But look underneath the words, and you'll find a sagging feeling as energy for the project sinks. What started out as a game worth playing, and a goal worth playing for, has been reduced to a series of — let's face it — chores.

Over the years I've asked a number of people to visualize and describe their border-crossing experience. This is what they say:

- I'm standing at the beach. It's a warm summer day. I close my eyes as I move toward the water. I think it's going to be warm and gentle. Suddenly I'm hit with a cold wave. It takes my breath away.

- I'm running across a field that suddenly turns into waist-high jelly, making every move forward a supreme effort.

- I'm making a soufflé over and over again, but no matter how hard I try, it doesn't want to rise.

- I'm a runner, showing up for a 10K, suddenly realizing that I brought the wrong shoes because there are more hills on this route than I planned for.

Each of us has a personal picture of what it's like at the border, but for all of us, the border is uncomfortable. The fact is that bringing an idea into physical reality almost always requires much more energy than we thought it would. This need for increased energy at the border is obvious when we look at rocket science. Rockets burn up most of their fuel during liftoff. When a space shuttle launches, it is amazing to see how much fuel is consumed during the first few seconds. For a few moments you see billowy smoke and steam at the base of the rocket, and it looks as though nothing is happening. Finally, there is the faintest shudder, almost imperceptible at first, as the rocket begins to move. It picks up momentum as it pushes through the inertia and begins to climb.

The same principle of liftoff applies to the ideas we want to launch. No matter how we strategize and prepare, physical reality is dense, and getting our project moving invariably takes much more energy than we'd planned.

This difference in energy between metaphysical and physical reality is just part of the story. We also bump into impermanence and unpredictability. Remember that English garden? In metaphysical reality you have a lovely idea and goal, maybe even a plan, a time line, and a budget. Then physical reality sets in, and you have to make moment-by-moment adjustments to deal with the unexpected. It takes longer than you thought. Or you go over budget. Or you discover you have to get a building permit for the gazebo you were going to throw together overnight. It goes on and on. If you've ever remodeled your home or held the hands of friends while they did, you know exactly what I mean.

People who bring forth their creative genius and begin adventures on a large scale meet up with Trouble at the Border on steroids. Consider George Lucas and the making of the *Star Wars* trilogy. Desert sands wrecking camera equipment, initial failures to get needed visual effects, running over budget — these were just for starters.

You can put your head down, grit your teeth, and forge your way through your border experience. You may get where you want to go, but you will probably be exhausted at the end — with a bad case of TMJ to boot. We are going for luminosity here. So we are looking for ways to cross the border with clarity, focus, ease, and grace.

When you learn to observe your own version of Trouble at the Border, you gain a great deal of power over it. You understand what's going on, so the fog lifts. And since you saw the border trouble coming, you don't waste a lot of energy flailing and fighting. You simply step back and observe, maintaining your clarity and focus.

Remember that observational gap the fish experienced when he jumped out of the water? An observational gap gives you breathing room. You may still need to pause, but you're much less likely to quit. So let's take a closer look at how your mind automatically reacts when you cross the border.

Monkey Mind: The Loyal Opposition

Monkey Mind is a term coined by Buddhists. I've used it in my work for about twenty years. It represents that aspect of the mind that is always chattering at us as it swings from doubt to worry and back to doubt again. Our Monkey Mind is fearful for our survival. It has no sense of proportion. Everything is big. Everything is a threat.

Monkey Mind has been with us forever, and it may have some survival value for us as a species. Look at it this way: we didn't have fangs or fur and couldn't run very far when we lived in caves or on the savanna. But we did have a mind that could conjecture about the future and plan for anything that might go wrong. That's Monkey Mind — a highly efficient, negative-possibility-forecasting mechanism. In physiological psychology this phenomenon is recognized to be produced by a small area in the brain called the amygdala, which triggers the fight, flight, or freeze response to danger. Bent upon keeping us out of danger, it kept us alert and ready to run or fight. The thing is, we don't need it much anymore except in real emergencies. But for Monkey Mind, almost everything new or different (including pursuing our dreams and goals) is an emergency.

Monkey Mind is insistent and highly personalized. It says the particular things that will make *you* pay attention, and it says them over and over again. What my mind says to me at the border is different from what your mind says to you. The images and the tone may be similar, but our self-limiting internal dialogues are very individual and personal. That's why when Monkey Mind starts chattering, it seems logical, undeniable, almost seductive. Some twelve-step programs describe this aspect of the mind as "cunning, baffling, and powerful."

Right now, in the interest of lifting the fog from your hero's path, let's observe your Monkey Mind thoughts. Once again, if you can observe what shows up for you at the border, you'll gain some power. If you can anticipate it and then observe it, you won't have to waste time and energy trying to make it go away or worrying that it means something is wrong.

Monkey Mind always greets us at the beginning of our adventures. In *The Wizard of Oz*, Dorothy and her friends enter the witch's forest. At the entrance to the forest a small sign reads, "I'd turn back if I were you." So says Monkey Mind, but the heroes continue on their journey.

The table on pages 59–62 lists common manifestations of Monkey Mind. I call them Monkey Mind symptoms. Beside each symptom are statements that exemplify the symptom. As you read, get a piece of paper and write down the symptom(s) most familiar to you, followed by a short statement describing how you demonstrate that symptom. (As you start, if you hear something in your head that says, "I don't know which ones are familiar!" that would be symptom number 1, "Being vague.")

Before turning to the list of Monkey Mind symptoms, let me highlight some of my recurring ones:

- Being a victim or martyr, as in, "No one understands just how hard I work."

- Comparing yourself to others, as in, "Other people have an easier time exercising than I do."

- Either-or thinking, as in, "Either I dance like a pro, or I won't take ballroom dancing lessons."

Be compassionate with yourself as you do this, and note that I'm not asking you to analyze *why* you have these symptoms. That kicks up the fog, remember? Just notice which symptoms ring a bell.

After you've read the list of symptoms and taken notes on how they sound in your head, take another piece of paper. Think about something you've always wanted to do or have but just haven't gotten to yet. Make it as specific as possible. Is there a project you want to tackle, a trip you want to take, a spiritual practice or sport you want to take up, or a job you want to go for? Look for something that's been on the sidelines, just waiting for your attention.

Put whatever it is as a title at the top of the paper. Next, jot down all the thoughts that come up about why you haven't done it or accomplished it. Get real with this. After about two or three minutes of writing, turn to the Monkey Mind symptoms list. Put what you wrote next to it, and see if additional symptoms start to sound familiar. Add these to the first piece of paper, where you made that initial list of your symptoms.

MONKEY MIND SYMPTOMS LAUNDRY LIST	
MONKEY MIND SYMPTOM	EXAMPLES
1. Being vague	• I think I understand what I need to do next, but I'm really not sure. • Maybe I'll do it sometime next month. • I just want my life to be better. Do I really need goals?
2. Scarcity thoughts	• Things are never going to get any better. • I don't have enough brains, money, time, creativity, etc., to do it.
3. Talking of the past or the future as if it is the present	• I've been down this road before. • It hasn't changed in the past, why would it in the future?
4. Defensiveness	• What do you mean, I'm not trying? I'm trying harder than you think! • I am *not* being defensive! I just don't like your tone of voice!
5. Taking things personally	• I am looking for more clients, but I just heard *no* so many times, I stopped calling. • I can't believe she talked to me that way.
6. Comparing yourself to others	• I'll never be as good as the other people in my department. • No one else could possibly have the same worries; they sail through this.
7. Resignation	• It's just too hard, and I'm not sure it serves people anyway. • This won't make a difference; things might as well just stay the way they are. • It's the same ol' same ol'.

MONKEY MIND SYMPTOMS LAUNDRY LIST (*Continued*)		
	MONKEY MIND SYMPTOM	EXAMPLES
8.	Being a victim or martyr	• I tried so hard and gave so much, but nobody responded. • When you reach a certain age, no one will hire you. • I wanted to go for it, but nobody helped me.
9.	Either-or thinking	• If I don't have five clients by next week, I might as well just give up. • Either I get to use my credit card, or I'll feel deprived.
10.	Making excuses	• I couldn't make it because I had more important things to do. • I would have gotten that project in, but the email system went down.
11.	Justification	• I wasn't going to let going for this goal ruin my weekend, so that's why I didn't make any calls. • I know I said I'd write three pages today, but I'm nurturing myself instead.
12.	Rationalization	• I would like to do this, but you must understand I wear many hats and have a lot of pressure. • Look, everyone speeds, so I'm sure ten miles per hour over the speed limit is built into the system.
13.	Fragmentation	• There's a part of me that doesn't have a clue. • If I can pull all the pieces floating around in my head together, then I'll be okay. • I can't help it: part of me just really wants to blow this off.

MONKEY MIND SYMPTOMS LAUNDRY LIST (*Continued*)	
MONKEY MIND SYMPTOM	EXAMPLES
14. Deflecting: Telling a joke to derail a conversation or divert attention from you	• Hey, I know I have money. There are checks in my checkbook. • I know I said I'd cut down on sugar. I didn't really want that hot fudge sundae. The devil made me do it!
15. Solidifying: Treating an abstract concept or metaphor as though it were an object in physical reality	• My opinion is rock solid. • I have a real bad case of low self-esteem. • I would write more, but I have writer's block.
16. Impulsiveness	• I want what I want, and I want it now! • I'm quitting my job tomorrow to throw myself into starting a coaching business. • I just had to buy lots of new office furniture. I want to start off right!
17. Qualifying statements	• Well, maybe if I get enough time I could finish that project. • If it seems right, I could probably ask for some support to do this. • I think I might be able to call you next week. I'll try.
18. Complaining/Petulance	• I do fine on my own. Everyone else holds me up because they're too slow. • There's too much pressure. That's why I'm failing. • If I do what I'm supposed to, why doesn't it turn out the way I thought it should? After all, I did my part, didn't I?

MONKEY MIND SYMPTOMS LAUNDRY LIST (*Continued*)	
MONKEY MIND SYMPTOM	EXAMPLES
19. The "Metafizzle"	• I know why this is so hard: it's a sign from Spirit that I'm not supposed to do it. • If I were meant to do this, it would be easier. • I guess I'm just not in harmony with my life; that's why it's not going the way I planned.
20. Being Paranoid	• She doesn't understand what I'm saying. She obviously doesn't care. • Nobody listens to me. They think I don't have anything to say. • Why am I out of the loop on that email? Don't they value my input?

Leave this aside for at least a day. After that, come back to it in the following way:

1. Tell at least one friend what your symptoms are. You're doing this as a way of getting used to observing them.

2. Listen for any of the Monkey Mind symptoms in your thoughts or in what you say out loud over the next week.

3. Do nothing more with them. Remember, no analyzing. You are just observing.

If you are like many who learn to name and observe their Monkey Mind symptoms, you'll discover that some of them have been with you for years. Even though they feel fresh each time they turn up, you'll see that they haven't changed much, no matter what the situation or goal. This is especially true if that goal required you to learn some new skills. Remember, one of the features of a game worth playing is the chance that you might lose. That's a big trigger for Monkey Mind — doing something that involves a risk.

Continue to observe Monkey Mind without doing anything else. In the next chapter you'll learn how to shift the focus of your attention to something more interesting — your goals and dreams — but right now, clarity is more than enough.

How to Tell the Difference between Monkey Mind and Your Voice of Wisdom

Clarity entails tuning in to our inner guidance systems. But how can we know when our voice of wisdom is speaking or when we're just having another Monkey Mind conversation? Of course Monkey Mind wants us to think it is our inner wisdom. Cultivating our powers of observation will help us here as well.

In general, Monkey Mind has one or more of the following qualities:

- It is insistent, as in "Listen to me *now*."
- It is survival oriented: the body tenses.
- There is a sense of dread or impending doom.
- It is defensive (experiences feedback as accusation).
- It is humorless except if using humor for deflection.

Your voice of wisdom, by contrast, has some of these qualities:

- It is compassionate, toward both you and others.
- It is spacious; your heart relaxes.

- There is some gentle good humor about yourself or the situation.

- There is generosity of spirit present, a kind, open-hearted view of people and situations.

- There is the sense that all is well.

Monkey Mind tends to chatter insistently and loudly in your ear. Your voice of wisdom speaks softly because it knows that if you don't learn whatever lesson is in front of you right now, you will do so in the future. Learning to observe rather than engage with Monkey Mind turns down its volume — and lets your inner wisdom get a word in edgewise.

Let's recap what we've learned about clarity.

We've explored our own fog-generating mechanisms and realized that many of the ways we've sought to navigate this hazard have only produced more haze. We've recognized the value of observing rather than analyzing when going for luminosity. Analyzing why we think the way we do can keep us in the same mode of thought that generated the fog. Observation lifts us above it.

We've seen that structuring goals as games worth playing — worth playing because they embody our Life's Intentions — harnesses our energies and points us toward luminosity. This is because of, and not in spite of, the rules of the game and the nature of physical and metaphysical reality.

And we've learned that to realize your heart's dreams and your mind's ideas, you must learn not to be stopped at the border between the metaphysical and the physical. You can expect that physical reality is going to push back at you when you begin to take action to attain a goal. It is a sign that you are on the right track. There is nothing wrong. You are experiencing what countless others have experienced through the ages; the game has begun.

If you take this principle to heart, you'll also see that when you are going for a goal or dream and you hear Monkey Mind, this too is a sign that you're on the right track. You are up to something big. There is nothing whatsoever wrong with you or your dream; Monkey Mind is simply giving you a signal that you are going into unpredictable territory toward a goal that's important to you. That is all — and that is a good thing!

The crucial thing to remember is this: if you listen to your Monkey Mind, become distracted, and stop yourself at the border, you are rewarding and empowering it. It will only get louder and stronger next time around. Instead, get to know your own personal Monkey Mind routines so that you can anticipate and observe them. Then when Monkey Mind starts chattering, you aren't blindsided, knocked down, or detoured. You can simply nod, wave, and say, "Thank you for sharing!" as you stay in the game and on your path.

Strengthening Focus

CHAPTER fiVE

You Already Are
Who You Are Willing to Be

*Your Life's Intentions are your blueprint
for focused, luminous action.*

*Vision without action is a daydream. Action without vision is
a nightmare.*

— Japanese proverb

Sometimes an experience can be so exquisitely sweet that you
think if your life were to end at that moment you'd feel complete. This isn't morbid. It's a sign that you know you are doing
exactly what you are meant to do. In that moment you are complete down to your bones.

Sometimes it's difficult to discover what you are meant to
do, especially when you're buffeted by the density, impermanence, and unpredictability of physical reality — and with
Monkey Mind screeching over your shoulder. What you need
is a touchstone, a way to bring certainty to the swirl of physical
reality, on one hand, and the changing landscape of your
thoughts and feelings, on the other. And that's why it's important to know and focus on your Life's Intentions.

Here's what I mean. Kurt is a chaplain at a Midwest hospital, and he told me the following: "One of my Life's Intentions is to be an effective healer. Two weeks ago I visited a man in the hospital on the evening before his coronary bypass surgery. His face was pale. He was scared. As it turned out, he got through the operation just fine. But on the night that I visited, he wanted to tell his family how much he loved them without making them too anxious or making it seem like he was taking his leave of them. With his permission, I led them all through a process that helped them say exactly how much they loved and cherished each other. They cried and hugged. There was so much joy in the room! It made my heart open up just to see the looks on their faces. Afterward, I thought that if *I* were to die right then, it would be okay because I had done what I entered this field to do."

We touched upon the concept of Life's Intentions in chapter 3. Now I'm going to ask you to fill out a Life's Intentions Inventory so that you can uncover the intentions that are important to you. This inventory represents work done with thousands of people over the past twenty-five years. In the beginning, before the inventory was developed, I would ask seminar participants what they wanted to be known for during their lifetime. It was a way for each one to see what mattered most to them in life. We'd start with a visualization process in which they'd be eavesdropping on friends who were planning a tribute for them at a surprise birthday party. I asked, "What would you want your friends and loved ones to say about you?" After some nervous laughter, people would come up with certain qualities that reflected not so much what they *did* as who they *were*.

As we would talk about these ways of being, the room would get lighter and everyone would relax and begin to smile. It was as though we all took a deep breath together. The collective Monkey Mind would calm down. That's when it dawned on me that this is a way to look directly into the heart of who we really are. Just talking about these qualities gives us a sense that all is well. I began to call them Life's Intentions. This is because an intention is a direction, aim, or purpose. The more we talked about them, the more we could see that these qualities gave a sense of meaning and purpose around which we could organize our lives.

Your Life's Intentions are the purposes you have come here to live *from*. They are intrinsic to who you are. You may therefore use them as a stable seat upon which you can sit as you look out into the shifting landscape of your life. At the same time, they are the blueprints for action that guarantee luminosity along your hero's path.

You will be drawn to some Life's Intentions and not to others. This is as it should be. Everyone has a number of them, and many remain fairly constant over time. Since these qualities live in metaphysical reality, they are not affected by the density, impermanence, and unpredictability of physical reality. In addition, these Life's Intentions can still be yours no matter what you think or feel about yourself at any given moment. For these reasons, you don't have to worry about them in any way. All you need to do is look for ways to demonstrate them in physical reality.

Take the Life's Intentions Inventory on page 73, and you will become absolutely clear about what is important to you. You will gain the structure — and focus — needed to create games worth playing.

Taking the Life's Intention's Inventory

In order to complete this inventory, you'll need a pen and a three-by-five card. But first, read each intention in the inventory. You will see that the intentions don't point to specific thoughts, feelings, or actions. Instead, every item in the Life's Intentions Inventory reflects a way of being. And each is precise. Once you have read each one, go back through the inventory and fill it out according to the instructions.

Give yourself a moment to take a deep breath before you go on. As you focus upon your most important Life's Intentions, you begin to reorient yourself to fundamental values and desires that transcend your everyday thoughts and feelings. You may experience a sense of possibility and promise. Those who spend a few moments regarding their most important Life's Intentions often report a subtle shift in their energy. They feel somehow lighter, more energized.

Return to the Life's Intentions that you scored at 4 or 5. Please list them on that three-by-five card. I'm going to ask you to carry this card with you for one day and look at it at least three times. That's all. Let yourself rest in the breathing room that is created when you look at your list.

When you look at the list of Life's Intentions that are currently at a 4 or 5, you may find that some have been with you forever. For instance, as long as I can remember, "To be an adventurer" has been a 5 for me. "To be a successful entrepreneur" has been important for the past twenty years while "To be an effective mentor" has been on my radar for about five years. In addition, you may see that your Life's Intentions are all related in some way. This is because each one points to a different aspect of the same human being: you.

LIFE'S INTENTIONS INVENTORY

Read through the intentions listed on the left. Then go back through the list, marking them according to their importance to you; five (5) is "very important" and one (1) is "relatively unimportant." In the blank line at the bottom, you may add an intention that is important to you but not listed. Please remember that this is only a snapshot in time, a reflection of where you are now. Your rating of these intentions could change at a later date.

MY INTENTIONS ARE TO BE:	1	2	3	4	5
Financially successful					
Physically fit and healthy					
A successful artist or sculptor					
A successful musician or composer					
A successful author, playwright, poet					
A contributor to my community					
A loving family member (mother, husband, partner, cousin, etc.)					
Spiritually developing					
A well-respected professional					
An effective teacher					
Well educated					
A creator of beauty					
An effective coach					
An effective healer					
Well traveled					
An effective mentor					
A successful entrepreneur					
An adventurer					
An effective therapist					
An effective minister					
A visionary leader					
A successful communicator					
A generous friend					
A successful team player					

Glancing at your Life's Intentions list, don't worry if you first feel relief and then immediately feel regret because you haven't done enough about some of them. That feeling of regret is a natural consequence of Monkey Mind awakening. Remember, Monkey Mind is the loyal opposition. It stands at the border between metaphysical and physical reality and shouts, "I'd turn back if I were you!" or, "It's too late for you!" Gently observe these thoughts without talking back to them or analyzing their roots, and then return your focus to those sweet Life's Intentions.

Bring your Life's Intentions list with you wherever you go for one day. Read over the list at least three times during the day — morning, midday, and before bed would be ideal. Get used to the company of your Life's Intentions. As you do this, you are constructing a foundation for creating games worth playing and goals worth playing for.

During this time, ask yourself the following:

- What do I experience as I look at the Life's Intentions that are important to me? How does my body feel? What thoughts come to mind?

- How would the quality of my life shift if conversations about these Life's Intentions replaced conversations about my doubts and worries?

You'll remember that in the last chapter I suggested you tell at least one person your favorite medley of Monkey Mind hits. Please do the same with your Life's Intentions list. Notice your energy when you talk with others about what's important to you. The best part of this is that you're making your Life's Intentions more real and familiar each time you bring them out into the light of day. You are letting them sink in.

Powering Up Your Life's Intentions

I'd like now to revisit a principle we discussed in chapter 1, *being willing*. We're going to add this to your Life's Intentions to give them a potent energetic boost.

As we explored, your most powerful gift, the one that puts you right on your hero's path, is your capacity to be willing — to say yes — no matter what Monkey Mind says and no matter what's going on in physical reality. Being willing is an effective affirmation. In fact, I would argue that it is the most potent of all affirmations.

The basic principle behind an affirmation is that it points to that which is true, right here, right now. It doesn't deal with the future because the future only occurs as a concept in physical reality. It also doesn't give rise to Monkey Mind because that aspect of our mind doesn't get activated when we tell the truth about the here and now. Monkey Mind might (probably *will*) comment on what we think or feel or remind us of a past experience or forecast something dire for the future, but it gains no toehold when we affirm what is true in this moment. A mundane example: when you see the sun and affirm, "The sun is shining," your Monkey Mind doesn't say, "No, it isn't." That's because you are telling the truth.

You may not know *how* to fulfill your Life's Intentions. You may think that you don't have the time, money, physical vitality, or creativity to do anything about them right now. You — and that Monkey Mind — may think that it would be impossible or dangerous to take action or that you'll feel foolish or terrified. But look beyond all of that "stuff." Are you nevertheless *willing*? I'm not asking you to say you're able or confident or to pretend that you are already halfway there. I'm just asking if you hear a yes in the midst of the fog and through the din of that chatty chimp.

Listen closely to yourself, and I'll bet you do hear that *yes!* (Note: The *yes* is not experienced as a weak voice. It's strong, gentle, and clear.) It is fundamental in your nature to be willing. It's the truth of who you really are. It's a reflection of your hero's heart. You may not have known you were willing. But if you get nothing else from this book, I want you to get that you have always been willing to say yes to your life. Even when you don't want to, you are nevertheless willing. It's when we don't know this about ourselves that we suffer.

Let's make this even more personally relevant. You are going to create a list of "fundamental affirmations." In chapter 1 I suggested you put the words "I am willing" on a three-by-five card and carry it with you for a few days. Take out that card now. Place it on the left, right next to that three-by-five card with your Life's Intentions. Read "I am willing" and then the first intention you listed, "To be _____," immediately after. So if you have a Life's Intention to be spiritually developing, you would read, "I am willing to be spiritually developing." Try this out with the first intention on your list.

What happens? You have just created a personal fundamental affirmation that is Monkey Mind–proof. That's because you are pointing to what is true, right here and now. The Life's Intentions that you rated a 4 or 5 are important to you. The moment you gave them that number, you said yes to them whether you knew it or not. When you put "I am willing" at the beginning and then read that fundamental affirmation, you clear the fog. You see the *yes* that has already been there waiting for you. Go ahead now and write, "I am willing," in front of all of the Life's Intentions on your list.

I suggest you carry this card with you for another few days. Read it several times a day to remind yourself of what's important to you. Use it to orient yourself before important events. Joel did just that, reading from his card of affirmations, "I am willing to be a successful entrepreneur," right before sitting down with a loan officer. The card calmed and focused him. He had prepared, and he got the loan. But just as important to Joel, and what the affirmation made possible, is that he got the loan with less stress — less wasted energy — than he thought possible. That's luminosity — clarity, focus, ease, and grace.

Play with your personal list. If one of your Life's Intentions is "To be a generous friend," it may be useful to read that affirmation before having lunch with a buddy. The same is true with "To be a loving partner" or "To be a creator of beauty."

It's so important that I'm going to reiterate: the secret to using affirmations in a way that works is to affirm *what you know to be true now, not what you hope will be true in the future.* Along these lines, affirm what is true in metaphysical reality. Don't use an affirmation to try to change anything in physical reality. Try this experiment to see what I mean:

- Say out loud the affirmation "I am wealthy. I have all the money I want."

  Now, say out loud "I am willing to be financially successful."

- Say out loud the affirmation "I have the relationship of my dreams."

  Now, say "I am willing to be a loving partner (husband, wife, lover)."

Fundamental affirmations, the second choice in each pair, point to what is true about you. Therefore, they get little or no

protest from Monkey Mind. They sit easy on the heart. You
don't have to train yourself to think a particular way, and you don't
have to put up a battle. You are not trying to change anything
in physical reality. Instead, you are reminding yourself of what
is important to you in a way that empowers you to construct a
game worth playing. Shift the focus of your attention toward
a fundamental affirmation that includes one of your Life's Intentions, and you have an opening for possibility.

By contrast, you'll hear from Monkey Mind when you try
to convince it — and yourself — that something not yet present
in physical reality actually exists. That's what we're doing with
the first choice in each pair. Our mind puts up a fight to prove
that it isn't true. Remember that Monkey Mind always looks
for whatever could go wrong in physical reality. When you tell
it that something is here now and it sees that this isn't true,
you're provoking mental mayhem.

It takes energy to deal with Monkey Mind in alarm. The
more we use affirmations to try to control physical reality or
thoughts and feelings, the louder Monkey Mind gets. Fundamental affirmations work from the inside out because you focus
first on what you are *willing* to bring to life. The energy you
save by not trying to change reality or restructure your
thoughts can be used instead to go for your dreams. That's energy efficiency!

Relax, You'll Never Reach Your Full Potential

Whenever I talk with people about living the lives they were
meant to live, someone says, "Tell me how I can reach my full
potential." That's when I answer, "Relax. You'll never do it."

Potential exists in metaphysical reality, and everything in metaphysical reality is present here and now as potential. The definition of potential is:

- Possible but not yet realized

- The capacity or ability for future development or achievement

- Probable, likely, budding, promise, the makings

Potential is that which is not yet realized in physical reality. By definition, then, you can't ever reach your full potential. This is good news. Haven't you had a secretly sinking feeling whenever you thought that you had to reach your full potential? That's because deep inside, where your voice of wisdom lives, you know that it's never going to happen. It isn't supposed to. When you reach your full potential, it's no longer potential. What you *can* do, though, is dance with potential in metaphysical reality in order to bring something into being in physical reality.

Look at it this way: you have one foot in physical reality and the other in metaphysical reality. You bridge the gap by seeing what's important to you in metaphysical reality while systematically going about making it happen in physical reality. That's where your excitement comes from. Potential is all about the *possibility* for something to occur in physical reality. You'll never run out of possibilities. Therefore, you'll never reach your potential.

Now, in terms of metaphysical reality, *you already are who you are willing to be*. If you are willing "To be a generous friend," it means you already are one in possibility. That's because in order for you to want to be a generous friend — to conceive the thought or write it down on paper — you must know what it means to be one. You may have seen someone acknowledging their friend or giving them a gift or being kind. You recognize it as generosity. The blueprint already exists inside of you. All you need to do is demonstrate being a generous friend in physical reality. You bring it into the light of day where it can be measured and treasured.

The same holds for "To be financially successful," "To be physically fit and healthy," and all the rest of your Life's Intentions. They already exist inside of you as potential. This is why you may have noticed your heart open when you put "I am willing" in front of them.

Are you willing to see that all of those Life's Intentions you listed describe an aspect of who you are? In this way you already are who you are willing to be. You already are a generous friend, physically fit and healthy, an adventurer, or spiritually developing. The blueprints exist inside of you. All you need do is demonstrate them.

Let this sink in. What I have just written has taken me years to appreciate. I used to gravitate toward seeing what was *wrong* with me instead of what was inherently *right*. I would look to the future for what I might become rather than to the present for who I already was. Whenever I did this there would always be a tightening around my heart along with the worry that I just might not get there. I might fall short and not get better.

As I worked with those who uncovered their Life's Intentions, I watched their faces light up with joy. They were coming home to themselves. It dawned on me that our hearts get full when our conversations reflect who we really are. In contrast, when we talk of our worries about who we may never become, our hearts tighten.

We are all here to take the ideas that excite us and accomplish them through action. We all yearn to contribute something of ourselves, to know that our lives have made a difference to our family, friends, and community. The ideas that we find most exhilarating are those that reflect one or more of our Life's Intentions. They speak to us clearly of the contributions we're here to make. That focus brings comfort and gives direction. We see inside ourselves that which is already whole and complete, just waiting to be expressed. We can breathe into life, knowing that all is well.

Getting Familiar with Your Life's Intentions

By constructing your Life's Intentions affirmation list, you have given yourself permission to see clearly who you are in your hero's heart. Remember, for the next three or four days, all I ask is that you carry the card around and look at it several times a day. As you do, you might notice that you're pulled to look at specific ways you might demonstrate your intentions. We got our feet wet with this kind of goal setting in chapter 3. But right now, let's focus on really getting to know these intentions — recognizing, affirming, solidifying the foundation.

Just try on your Life's Intentions. Get used to their texture. Let them come to fit you like a favorite pair of comfy shoes. Walk around in them. Notice what happens to your energy as you observe your Life's Intentions list. Give yourself the pleasure or relief of seeing them.

Spend time with your Life's Intentions, and you will see that they both are and are not about you. By that I mean they give you the opportunity to do something both important to you and of benefit to others. Life's Intentions ask you to take your attention off those routine worries and put it onto what you're here to do with your life. The worries may never go away; they don't have to. You have found something more interesting upon which to focus your energy. You are orienting yourself toward luminosity, as a sunflower to the sun. And if you once waited for life to clear up, you now find yourself joyously running out onto your playing field — with clarity, focus, ease, and grace.

CHAPTER SIX

Your Standards of Integrity

It's not just what *you do but* how *you do it.*

Make a careful list of all things done to you that you abhorred. Don't do them to others, ever. Make another list of things done for you that you loved. Do them for others, always.

— Dee Hock, author of *Birth of the Chaordic Age*,
in *Fast Company* magazine

It has been said that each of us operates on three levels. The first is who we *pretend* to be. It's our cover. You see it all the time at professional meetings, civic events, and any gathering where people don't know each other very well. We want to make a favorable impression. It's natural. Almost everyone takes cover by pretending, especially in new situations.

Underneath who we pretend to be — and probably the reason for the pretense itself — is who we're *worried* we are. This is where our doubts about ourselves live. Everyone has these doubts. We worry that we're overdressed or underdressed or that we won't come up with a brilliant statement or make people laugh. We're afraid we don't have what it takes to contribute to the situation or that someone else could handle it all so much more brilliantly than we ever could.

Monkey Mind lives on both these levels, hopping back and forth. In fact, try this: go back over the Monkey Mind symptoms in chapter 4. Take a minute and categorize a few of them: are they mostly about pretense or worry or both? For example, you can see how the symptom "Comparing yourself to others" could be used either to foster the pretense of looking good or the worry about not looking good enough.

If we go still deeper, though, the third aspect of ourselves lives at the center: who we *really* are. This is all about the hero's heart. The qualities and attributes that describe who we are in our heart transcend all those thoughts and concerns about ourselves. They exist apart from what we think and feel in the moment.

Your Life's Intentions fall into this category since they represent what is most important to you. If you look right now at the ones that you scored at least 4 or 5, you'll see they are like beacons of light. They shine through any fog that Monkey Mind could generate.

If you can access who you really are quickly and easily, you'll spend less time and energy pretending to be someone, on the one hand, and being worried about who you are, on the other. Focusing on your Life's Intentions cuts through the layers of pretense and worry. You can use your Life's Intentions to guide you straight to your hero's heart. What is the benefit of discovering that hero's heart? It provides more clarity. It reminds me of a remark that Lily Tomlin made: "I always wanted to be someone, but now I realize I should have been more specific."

Most of us, however, accompanied by Monkey Mind, spend a lot of time dancing between pretense and worry. I was definitely doing the Monkey Mind two-step as I anticipated my ten-year high school reunion. Two weeks before the event, I was thinking about how I couldn't fit into the Levi's I'd worn when I was sixteen. Any pretense that my body hadn't changed was impossible. I arrived on campus wearing slacks two full sizes bigger and worried that I wouldn't hear a soothing "Maria, you haven't changed a bit!" The irony is that my beloved boarding school was located in Sedona, Arizona, known for its spiritual energy. The red rocks there are majestic, and the area is at once peaceful and uplifting — unless you're busy pretending and worrying.

I wish I'd known then about the Life's Intentions guidance system for getting to the hero's heart. The more consistently we access this system, the more likely we'll dance to the tunes that we find interesting in any situation. At least by the time I got to the next reunion I had learned to observe my pretending and worrying a lot more quickly. I could then shift the focus of my attention to something more interesting, like my Life's Intention "To be a generous friend."

Heroes for the Hero's Heart

Here is another focusing tool for creating luminous moments. Like awareness of your Life's Intentions, it will guide you as you create your games worth playing and goals worth playing for. You will be making a list of the people who have qualities or traits you admire.

This focusing tool begins with the following questions:

Whom do you admire? Who inspires you? I have asked these
of thousands of people over the years. Some people had clear
and ready answers, while others had to think about it for a
while. But almost always, searching for role models, inspiring
mentors, or personal heroes brought a calm look and lifted
spirit, much as looking at one's Life's Intentions does.

So get a clean piece of paper. Then turn back to the Life's
Intentions Inventory in chapter 5, and find the intentions that
are important to you, that scored 4 or 5. For example, you might
place a high value on "To be spiritually developing." Write that
down on your new piece of paper.

Next, think of people who inspire you because they demonstrate that Life's Intention in physical reality. If you find even
one person who fills the bill, that's good. Looking at another
Life's Intention, pick other people who embody it in what they
do. After this, either go on to other Life's Intentions or just
make a list of people who have at least one or more qualities
you admire. They could be living or not, people you know or
public figures, people you have either met or read about. They
could be in your family or circle of friends or people who have
mentored you during important times in your life. Don't think
about the specific qualities that you might admire in these
people at this point. That comes later. Right now, focus upon
the people.

Take your time with this list. Simply looking at who inspires you can begin to shift your energy. You might notice your
body relaxing or your heart opening as you think about them.
You may experience a sense of gratitude that there really are
people with these qualities. Give yourself a moment to absorb
the list before going further.

I've talked with many people over the years who have done great things in their lifetimes. They've founded successful churches, owned thriving land development businesses, directed state agencies with multibillion-dollar budgets, or become well-known artists, authors, and interviewers. When I asked each of these successful people to tell me about people they admired, almost every one could give me a list right on the spot. Boom! No hesitation. These accomplished people were in touch with their appreciation for the greatness in others.

Randall put it this way: "I know it might sound odd, but sometimes before an important meeting, I'll ask myself, 'How would Thomas Jefferson handle this?' I may not get a specific answer, but somehow just asking that question puts me on a different wavelength. I calm down. My thoughts get clearer. I'm not 'channeling' Thomas Jefferson, it's just that when I think about him and how brilliantly he thought, *I* suddenly feel smarter."

What Your Admiration of Others Says about You

Just as with Randall and other successful people, it's no accident that you chose the specific people you admire. There are certain qualities they possess that resonate within you. This says as much about you as it does about them.

Let's get more specific now about the qualities that you admire in those people you listed earlier.

Start with the first person on your list. Think about what the specific attributes are that, when you think of them, open your heart. Below are words that have been culled from thousands who have already done this process. It's a partial list, a way to get you started. Notice that the words are adjectives. They describe the person. They are not nouns, like the word *loyalty*. I recommend adjectives for a reason. Just as we saw with the word *willingness*, we experience nouns as occurring outside of us. For example, the phrase "I have loyalty" is clearly less powerful than "I am loyal."

ATTRIBUTE LIST

Appreciative	Engaging	Loyal
Attentive	Enthusiastic	Mindful
Authentic	Focused	Persistent
Aware	Friendly	Reliable
Brilliant	Generous	Spiritual
Clear	Gentle	Steadfast
Compassionate	Genuine	Supportive
Conscious	Grateful	Thorough
Courageous	Healing	Thoughtful
Creative	Humble	Trustworthy
Decisive	Inspiring	Truthful
Dedicated	Intelligent	Uplifting
Dependable	Kind	Visionary
Encouraging	Loving	Vital

Once again, these are only examples of the attributes you could find that are important to you. As you read through this list, other qualities may come to mind. So, keeping your focus on that first person on your list, write down specifically what you admire about that person. You can put as few or as many as you wish. Do this with the next person. What do you appreciate about him or her? Write the attributes down. If any of them are the same as the previous person's, then all you have to do is make a check mark to indicate that this quality showed up again. At the end you'll have an inventory of admirable characteristics, some of them followed by a row of check marks. It may look something like this:

Compassionate ✓✓✓

Inspiring ✓✓

Visionary ✓✓✓✓

Intelligent ✓✓

Loyal ✓✓✓

Trustworthy ✓✓✓✓✓✓✓

Creative ✓✓✓

It doesn't matter how many qualities you listed or how many check marks (if any) show up after each one. What's essential is that you have collected a group of traits that express what you admire in other people. Please print this list on a three-by-five card, much as you did your Life's Intentions. Leave a little margin at both the top and bottom of the list. If you have a longer list than the one above, you may need to make a few columns. Just make sure to get all the qualities on one side.

Look again at the list of attributes you prepared. They sing to your heart, don't they? That's because they are a reflection of who *you* really are.

Yes, what you wrote is a description of yourself. You will always know who *you* really are by the qualities you admire in others. Remember the axiom that we don't like in others the things that we don't like in ourselves? Well, the opposite is also true: *you value in others the qualities that lie within you.*

This is true by the same mechanism we discussed in the last

chapter: if you are willing to be, say, a generous friend, you already know what that means; a generous friend blueprint exists within you. Similarly, if you admire someone who is compassionate, you must know what being compassionate means. Borrowing a metaphor from biochemistry, you've got to have a receptor site for compassion in order to recognize and value compassion. It has a place to cling to in your heart.

Let this in. Read the attributes inventory you created, and come home to *yourself*.

The attributes you listed are your Standards of Integrity. Standards are principles, and principles are guidelines you can use, like your Life's Intentions, to lift the fog from your path. Integrity is the state of being complete, whole, and sound. Therefore, your Standards of Integrity are principles that guide you to wake up to your true nature. You can focus on them when everything around you is in flux. They reflect what endures, no matter the situation or circumstance.

Look again at your three-by-five Standards of Integrity card. Above the list of qualities, please write, "These are my standards of integrity. I am:" And at the bottom of the card, write, "I know these are mine because I see them in others." Your list may be shorter or longer, but your card will now look more or less like this:

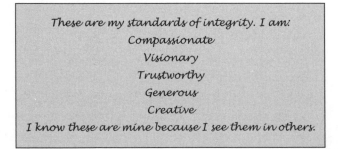

These are my standards of integrity. I am:
Compassionate
Visionary
Trustworthy
Generous
Creative
I know these are mine because I see them in others.

The next thing to do is to get this card laminated. You will be using it more as you move through this book.

Your Luminosity Quotient

You now have two guidelines that you can use to create luminosity in everyday life. First, your Life's Intentions show which games you find worth playing. They reflect what you're up to in your life. If you haven't done it yet, take a three-by-five card and list all the Life's Intentions from the previous chapter that scored 4 or 5 for you. Write "I am willing" in front of each. Laminate it, just as you did the Standards of Integrity card.

Your Standards of Integrity show you *how* to play those games in order to bring about the best results. They speak of those specific and vital attributes that lie within you, waiting to be demonstrated in physical reality.

Remember, *anyone* can be busy, but the busy life isn't the successful life. We want quality here. We want luminosity — the sense of possibility and promise we feel when we absolutely know that all is well and that we're doing what we're meant to be doing, right here, right now. We reach luminosity through a different quality of action — clarity, focus, ease, and grace *in action*.

Let's put your Standards of Integrity to work in a pragmatic way in order to demonstrate a different quality of action. Take your Standards of Integrity card with you for the next three days. Look at it right before your next staff meeting, family get-together, session with a client, or wherever you are willing to experiment. When you reach a point where you need to make a decision, give someone feedback, or voice your point of view, glance first at that card and ask yourself, "How would someone with these attributes respond right now?"

This may seem like a small thing to do. It isn't. The smallest changes in your typical ways of interacting with other people can have great effects. In fact, small shifts often have bigger effects than drastic changes. People can deal with small, sweet shifts in behavior. They don't get thrown off. There's no drama.

Flor found this to be true in a very practical way. Flor works hard as the owner of a restaurant. She serves the best Mexican chile verde in town, from an old New Mexico family recipe. She did the Standards of Integrity exercise, took her card with her to work, and then told me this story: "At my restaurant we run on a very tight profit margin. That's why the crew and I were upset when we had to throw away an entire batch of chile verde because someone forgot to refrigerate it the night before. I wasn't happy. Not one bit. But I had my Standards of Integrity card with me. While we stood around the kitchen counter, I snuck a peak. *Generous* and *compassionate* were on there. It sounds funny, but it's like the words were glowing out at me. I asked myself how a compassionate and generous person would handle this situation. The first thing I noticed was that I wasn't angry anymore. I said, 'Let's not blame any one person since all of us were asleep on this one.' Before I knew it, we had looked at lessons learned, and someone had come up with a system so that this wouldn't happen again. We solved the problem. It was worth the cost of the chile to see the team working as a unit together!"

Small changes can produce big effects. I've heard many stories over the years that reflect the miracles that can happen when you begin to demonstrate who you really are in everyday interactions with others. Remember, miracles are about our perceptions being made finer so that we can see and hear what has always been around us.

As you carry your Standards of Integrity card with you for the next three days, this is what I suggest you look for:

- When you are mindfully demonstrating your Standards of Integrity, notice if your body relaxes or your heart seems to open. Look at whether or not you have more energy or more of a sense of gentle humor in situations that used to stress you.

- Look at how others react when you demonstrate your Standards of Integrity. See whether or not they relax, smile more, become more creative, or just seem to have an easier time around you. If you work with a group, see if there is more collaboration in your presence or if the team comes to creative solutions a little more easily.

Experimenting with your Standards of Integrity in this way brings shifts, a new quality of energy. I want to look more closely at this energy, and it will entail exploring an aspect of you that we normally don't talk about so it won't be easy to describe. Please bear with me; it's worthwhile.

Ontology: Who You Really Are

What are you thinking right now as you are reading? *Who* is thinking those thoughts? Is there something about you that's "bigger" than the thoughts you think? If not, how would you be able to observe the thoughts you're thinking? Let me illustrate these questions with an anecdote from my life.

When I was in psychoanalysis, training to become a psychoanalyst, I would lie on the analytic couch looking up at the acoustic tiles on the ceiling. Over the years I'd come to know every watermark, every pattern, on those nine square feet.

In most kinds of psychoanalysis, you free-associate, saying essentially everything that comes into your head and then trying to make sense of these thoughts, to relate them to what's going on at a deeper level. Some of the time the insights I got this way were useful, but much of the time my thoughts recycled themselves. This went on for years.

One day I had an epiphany. It was disturbing, and it wouldn't go away. No matter what I talked about in that office, I came back to these questions: "Is that all I am — just one thought or feeling after another? Isn't there something more to me?"

About that time, I went to a personal growth seminar in Los Angeles. It was 1981, and the transformational movement was just starting to take hold. Suddenly I saw the possibility that I was more than those analytic mental productions. I heard the person leading the seminar asking the same questions I'd heard in my own head.

The following year was one of the most uncomfortable — and liberating — of my life. I didn't think the same way. For starters, I didn't take my every thought as the gospel truth. Now, it's very big for a psychoanalytically trained psychologist *not* to take thoughts and feelings seriously!

I tell you this because throughout this book I have been talking about the mind. Now, what is it to say, "I have a mind"?

Does the mind observe itself? To observe something, you have to get outside of it, and then you have to ask, "What lies outside the mind that could observe it?"

Ask yourself, "Who is thinking my thoughts and having my feelings?" The thoughts aren't having thoughts. The feelings aren't having feelings. If I say, "My brain," then I have to ask, "*What* is it that is observing I have a brain?"

You might answer that your ego is observing all of this. But even talking about the ego, you can wonder, "What is observing that I have an ego? *What* is even observing the word *I*?"

This can be disorienting. It's like Alice in the rabbit hole. Whenever you arrive at what you think is the final answer, the question comes back, "*Who* is observing what you just named?"

Let me offer a term that helped me through this conundrum. I learned it in that seminar in 1981: *ontology*. The word means different things to different people. For example, the philosopher Martin Heidegger talked in his writings about ontology as the study of existence.[1]

Back in the 1980s, as I read Heidegger, a door opened so that I could look at a possibility beyond my thoughts, feelings, and body sensations. But I had no clear way to take his philosophical principles and apply them in physical reality — and I needed guidelines for working out the small stuff in my everyday life.

Then I came across a definition of *ontology* from a metaphysical perspective. There are four branches of metaphysics: psychology, ontology, theology, and cosmology. Psychology is the study of our thoughts and feelings. Ontology is the study of being, in the sense of who we are spiritually. It's a compassionate and intimate look at who we are that includes the study of our true nature and what we're here to accomplish in life. Theology is the study of the various ways of seeing God, and cosmology is the study of the nature of the universe.

Over the past twenty-five years of my work, I discovered this: we have a natural desire to express who we truly are. It's in our heart of hearts. This is our pathway to luminosity, since we create luminous moments when we demonstrate who we are ontologically in everyday life.

There is a substantial difference between who you are psychologically and who you are ontologically. You gain the focus to create your games worth playing and goals worth playing for when you see clearly what this difference is.

We can describe who we are psychologically by looking at our thoughts, feelings, opinions, attitudes, states of mind, or body sensations. We know how to talk about ourselves in this way. We can describe what we think and feel in great detail, but for the most part our thoughts and feelings are transitory. They change almost with each breath we take, as anyone who has ever tried meditation will instantly agree.

At the center of who we really are is something much bigger than our psychological makeup. It doesn't change from moment to moment. It is a steady place inside us that lets emotions and thoughts wash over it like waves but remains essentially unchanged. This is our ontological nature.

While we can easily talk about who we are psychologically, it's impossible to describe ourselves directly in terms of our ontology. That's because every time we say something about ourselves as a definitive answer to the question "Who are you?" the next question that automatically pops up is, "And who just said those words?"

So if we can't talk directly about who we are from an ontological perspective — if it's not possible to look directly into the face of being — what *can* we do? This is where it gets very interesting. Let's borrow an analogy from quantum physics.

Quantum physics studies particles so small and elusive that it's difficult to measure them. It's also difficult to tell whether they have mass or are just vibrations of energy or whether they share the properties of both. One way scientists get a bead on them is by watching for their reflections on highly sensitive photographic surfaces.

We'll use a similar method to talk about your ontological nature. For while it is impossible to see directly into the nature of being, you can nevertheless see the *reflections* of being as they show up on the photographic plate of your heart. You know when you are in the presence of these ontological reflections because you have a sense that all is well — that you have come home to yourself. And that is precisely the experience people report when they discover their:

- Life's Intentions

- Standards of Integrity

- Capacity to be willing no matter what they think and feel

- Ability to observe rather than analyze

Just directing your gaze toward these four reflections of your true nature shifts your energy and causes your heart to open to the possibilities that surround you. That's why I suggest you carry your Life's Intentions and Standards of Integrity with you to look at on a daily basis.

You have a profound effect upon others when you demonstrate who you are ontologically. In your presence, others experience compassion, generosity of spirit, spaciousness, and a gentle good humor. Not only do you have a sense that all is well, they do too. This is the ideal playing field, the perfect place for your games worth playing and goals worth playing for — and *you* create this playing field by directing your focus.

In what comes next, you will learn how to focus on what is important to you. In shifting the focus of your attention from your psychological to your ontological nature, you gain access to a wellspring of wisdom from which you can draw no matter what's going on around you. You'll use your energy to get what truly matters to you. As a result, your dreams will become a reality, with more ease than you ever thought possible!

CHAPTER SEVEN

Draw Your Own Conclusions

*Gathering evidence for the conclusions you care about
makes your actions effective.*

*My life has been filled with terrible misfortune, most of which
never happened.*

— Michel de Montaigne

We all act on evidence that we're sure in the moment is accurate. But things don't always turn out the way we thought they would. Or, even worse, sometimes situations turn out the same worn-out, predictable, and boring way over and over again.

The point is that our conclusions about what's happening around us affect how we act, so we want to operate from conclusions that allow our actions to be effective — maybe even luminous.

The following incident brought this home for me. Alone one late summer afternoon, on the way back from a short hike in the California hills, I saw something brown and slithery looking in the distance. It was coiled in the middle of the path. A snake! I could see poison oak on either side of the trail, so there was no going around the snake. The sun was beginning to set. My heart beat fast. I saw images of myself up there all night, freezing and hungry. No one would know where I was.

I came closer, with caution. At about thirty feet, I saw the snake wasn't moving. At the same time, my perception about the shape began to change. Was it a snake or some other animal I'd never seen before? Finally, when I was about twenty feet away, it hit me. This wasn't a snake at all. It was a huge cow pie, dead center in the middle of the road! I laughed, suddenly glad no one was there to see how foolish I had been. My heart rate slowed as I hiked down the hill.

My reaction had been appropriate to what I had "seen." The perceived threat brought on a raised heartbeat and images of night on the trail alone. I could not have reacted otherwise. To pretend that I didn't see a snake when I thought I did would have been impossible. It got me thinking: How much of my life is spent reacting to what I think is really out there but may not be?

In *Blink: The Power of Thinking Without Thinking*, Malcolm Gladwell makes the compelling case that we are constantly reacting to conclusions we've drawn whether we are aware of them or not.[1] They dictate our choices and shape our behavior more than we know. Particularly striking is the fact that many conclusions are like reflexes; we don't control them. They have the automatic quality of a knee-jerk response.

But all is not lost. Through choosing how to direct the focus of your attention, you do have the power to ultimately determine your experience of life and how satisfying that experience will be.

If you want to change how you experience your life, it is *not* — I repeat *not* — necessary to change your thoughts. All you need to do is to shift your focus to those that interest you more, for example, that reflect your Life's Intentions and Standards of Integrity. This is no trivial distinction.

Why You Don't Have to Change Your Thoughts (Even if You Could)

First, is your brain busy? Try to make a tick mark for every thought you have in a two-minute period, and you'll be astounded at how many of them pass in front of you, like the clouds before the sun on a windy day. It's an endless parade.

If you really tried to change your thoughts, it could drive you crazy. How could you stop each thought marching in the parade long enough to change it? Think of the energy expenditure! You'd soon be exhausted and frustrated, and I can see the fog rolling in just thinking about this futile process.

You might say that instead of changing your thoughts, you simply won't think them. Good luck. This is equally difficult because your brain basically doesn't understand the word *don't*. To return to the example from chapter 2, for the next ten seconds, try *not* to think about a hot fudge sundae with nuts and whipped cream. Go ahead, *don't* think about it. What happens? You guessed it. Rows of hot fudge sundaes parade through your head.

This aspect of brain function — focusing upon the subject, even when it's preceded by a *don't* or *not* — is well understood by therapists who use hypnosis. For example, look at the following two phrases, and pick the one that would most clearly produce the intended result:

- Don't forget to take your car keys when you leave.

- Remember to take your car keys when you leave.

It's obvious, isn't it? The first suggestion puts "forget to take your keys" into your mind. The second, "remember to take your keys," is easier for the brain to follow and therefore more apt to influence your behavior in the desired manner.

It is difficult both to try to change a thought or conclusion and to ignore one you already have. Each strategy takes a lot of energy and gives few results. In addition, you become rigid and hemmed in by your thoughts, which seem to get louder as they repeat themselves over and over again.

That's because whatever you focus on repeats itself. So trying to change your thoughts keeps your focus on those thoughts, causing them to recycle. Ultimately more elegant, easy, and powerful than trying to change your thoughts is learning to shift the way you think them.

The work we've done up to now has given you clear reflections of who you really are in your heart of hearts. Now you're going to apply this to create results that will excite you as well as warm that heart of yours. It will be easier than you think — because you won't have to change your thoughts.

What you will learn instead is how to shift the focus of your attention from the conclusions that no longer interest you to the ones that do. And, as we shall see, shifting your attention has nothing whatsoever to do with changing those conclusions. As the energy of your attention is withdrawn, those old conclusions simply recede into the background.

In the Beginning Was the Conclusion

Let's take a look at the process we all use to create life experiences. The Four-Box Model illustrates the process. We start with the upper left corner, box 1.

THE FOUR-BOX MODEL

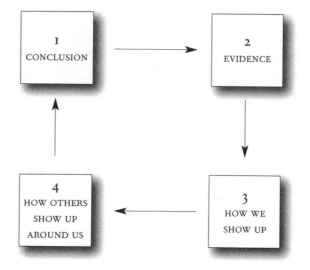

Box 1 is labeled Conclusion. Normally we think that a conclusion is an opinion we form *after* we've considered relevant facts or evidence. But here we put it first. In effect, we're saying, "In the beginning was the conclusion."

The mind is a conclusion-manufacturing machine. For example, it's common knowledge that people form conclusions about each other within one or two minutes. Malcolm Gladwell writes that these conclusions are often created in a matter of seconds. He calls it "thin slicing."[2] As I've worked with people over the years, I've noticed the following sequence:

1. A conclusion is like a reflex. It takes very little to set one off.

2. Once it's triggered, the brain only looks for evidence that will validate that conclusion.

3. Therefore, our evidence is automatically and predominantly determined by the triggered conclusion, *not the other way around*.

This power to generate quick conclusions about our environment may have helped us survive since prehistoric times. Since we're not as physically rugged as many animals, we have learned to size up situations and people quickly. This gives us an edge; once again, this is the amygdala in action.

The human brain is, in fact, wired for conclusions, even from a perceptual point of view. When you can't draw conclusions it is disorienting. To show you what I mean, imagine the following: You're in a room. Wherever you look — on the floor, ceiling, and walls — all you see is the kind of visual "snow" or static you'd get from a television with no reception. You hear no noise. The lights aren't glaring. Just that static, wherever you direct your gaze.

How long could you last in that room? You're facing no obvious threat, but your inability to draw perceptual conclusions, or gestalts as they're called in perceptual psychology, could make you very agitated.

So it becomes clear that we all gather evidence to support the conclusions that interest us. What's more, not everyone sees a situation in the same way, even when presented with the same "objective" facts. One place this becomes obvious is when listening to different members talk about the same family.

Take Jim, for example. We were talking about the four-box paradigm in a seminar, and he came up with the following: "Sometimes I think my brothers and I were born in different families. I mean that we don't see things the same way when we talk about our parents. My brother Pete is convinced that Dad would *argue* at the dinner table and *discourage* anyone from answering back. Me? My memory is that he was trying to *teach us how to debate* issues. In fact, that's why I think I did so well on the debate team in college."

In box 2 of the Four-Box Model, we look at the kind of evidence our conclusions lead us to find. For example, if you were to interview Jim and Pete separately, each could give you compelling facts that would substantiate his position. In fact, the brighter we are, the more detailed and deliciously descriptive our data becomes.

Imagine that you and I are working at the same office. We're friends. One day I come to you and say, "My boss is a jerk." You say, "Are you sure? Maybe he's just having a rough week. You know the IT system has been down."

The next thing I'm likely to do is give you evidence to support my "jerk" conclusion about my boss. It's natural because once I'm focused upon a conclusion — any conclusion — my brain is wired to automatically provide evidence for why that conclusion is correct. It's a matter of survival (so the mind thinks) to be correct about what it has deduced. This means that I'm not going to be interested in evidence that might contradict my assertion.

If you hear me out but still counter with something like, "I hear you, Maria. But as your friend, I still have to ask you if you're sure that he's not just having a rough few days," you'd be very brave. You would be challenging my conclusion, and I might relent but probably not without a struggle. It goes against the grain to reassess a conclusion. I am in the groove of my own evidence-gathering process.

Box 3 is about how you show up based on the evidence you're dealing with in the moment. You cannot help but act in ways that reflect the evidence you're focused upon. Getting back to the boss scenario, how am I most likely to act if I'm sure my boss is a jerk? How do I look to you as I give you my supporting evidence? Is there much generosity of spirit? Compassion? Spaciousness? What might my facial expressions convey? Am I especially empowering or inspiring to be with at that moment? Or am I showing up as judgmental and small-minded?

We are hardwired to react to what we perceive — be it real or not. Neurophysiological research shows that the brain often fails to distinguish between what is happening outside, in physical reality, and what's going on inside the brain itself. That's the principle behind guided visualizations: if you can create calming and pleasant scenes in your mind, your heart rate and other physiological measures will follow suit.

Box 4 is about how others show up around us. Let's take the scenario with my boss one step further. As I'm talking with you about him, he happens to enter the room. He looks at me. Predictably, I'm not thrilled to see him. He picks that up and walks out, or maybe he frowns before asking me to do something.

This causes me to give you an "I told you so" look. My original box 1 conclusion is validated. Case closed.

Let me be clear about the fact that I'm not discounting or excusing other people's behavior. The boss may well be doing what I say he's doing. His behavior could cause some people to label him as a jerk. But could there be another way to see it? We've all heard about — or experienced — situations in which we were sure about our assessment of another person, only to find out that his or her behavior could be seen in another light. I give you the Kit Kat story to illustrate this point.

Jane goes to London, sits down in a pub, and orders a cup of tea and a Kit Kat chocolate bar. A man sits down next to her, reaches over, and breaks off a section of the candy. A few minutes later he does this again, polishing off the chocolate.

Jane doesn't want to look like an unseasoned American tourist, and she's read that pubs are communal places. So she decides to bite her tongue — until the man orders a jelly doughnut and then gets up and takes it to another table, where he sits down next to another solitary woman.

Sure the man is about to harass another woman, Jane marches over to his table, grabs the doughnut, and takes a big bite. She then slams it down and makes her way out the door. Harrumph!

Trouble is that when Jane gets outside to her bus stop, she reaches into her purse for change — and finds her Kit Kat bar. She'd been poaching *his* all along — no doubt setting Anglo-American relations back a century or two.

Now back to my boss. Let's say I decide to turn over a new leaf. I don't want to show up small or mean-spirited toward him. I want to change my ways. Why is it so difficult to do this?

As our conversation progresses, I say to you, "Okay. Maybe you're right. I'll try something: for the rest of the day, no matter what he says to me, I'll be nice. I won't let him get to me."

That strategy may work for about an hour. Then my boss says something to me that sets in motion that first conclusion about being a jerk, and I'm off to the races gathering evidence, this time being doubly right because, after all, I did try to give him the benefit of the doubt.

This all happens because my conclusion — "my boss is a jerk" — never left the scene. It was still there, embedded in my words, "no matter what he says to me, I won't let him get to me." So, armed with a conclusion and no matter what I said I'd try, I was still gathering supporting evidence for that original conclusion. I couldn't help it. It is extremely difficult to change behavior in the face of the same old conclusion.

This four-box sequence is inevitable. You can't change the sequence, but you do have control over what you fill those boxes with. And that is the key to luminosity, as the following example shows.

In a workshop once, as we talked about the people we admire, Mother Teresa's name came up. A participant reminded us that Mother Teresa had often been quoted as saying that for her, every person with whom she came in contact literally *was* Christ, "in all of his distressing disguises." She dedicated her life to this view and held that it was true about everyone.

Mother Teresa's (extraordinary) vision of people was a box 1 conclusion — that each individual is the Christ. If you were dedicated to seeing everyone as Christ, we wondered, what would your box 2 evidence look like?

You'd see each person as having tremendous worth and value, we surmised. As Mother Teresa said, as you were washing the body of the sickest person, you'd be washing the body of Christ.

We looked next at box 3 and asked how someone who gathered evidence that everyone was Christ would show up. Joyous, inspired, and fiercely devoted to seeing that everyone experienced dignity, respect, and love at least once during his or her lifetime: that described Mother Teresa's mission and experience.

Finally, at box 4, how would others show up around a person with these conclusions? We imagined people would feel that all was well and would be healed in spirit. (I have heard people report that simply seeing a video of Mother Teresa walking or holding a baby opened their hearts.)

To confirm what we were saying, a person at the workshop remembered reading an article about Mother Teresa in which she talked to people who came to India to work with her. She told them not to come with sorrowful faces, that the people there didn't need pity. They needed love and respect. She wanted people who worked with her to express the joy that would go along with being in the presence of Christ.

I have now worked for a number of years with the four boxes and know that the following will shift us toward luminosity:

1. If you want to change your behavior, don't concentrate on the behavior itself.

2. Instead, shift the focus of your attention to a conclusion that interests you.

3. Your behavior will naturally and effortlessly shift to conform to the new evidence that this conclusion generates.

The next chapter goes into greater detail about how to shift the focus of your attention to conclusions that interest you. And I'll show you how it could apply to the "boss is a jerk" scenario.

But to give you an immediate sense of how it works, let's look at a conclusion that's both prevalent and frustrating for many of us: losing weight.

Jody had a major triumph in this area. She told me about how she used the four-box paradigm to transform her relationship with her body. At forty-two, she was bright, energetic, and disheartened. "I had gained and lost the same twenty pounds over and over again. Even my cellulite had déjà vu! The conclusion I had focused my attention upon for years was that I needed to lose weight. Looking at that conclusion, I now see that the 'lose' part didn't stand out as much as the 'weight' part. And that word *weight* was always on my mind.

"After looking at my Life's Intentions, I decided to shift the focus of my attention to the following fundamental affirmation: 'I am willing to be physically fit and healthy.' I wrote it on a three-by-five card and carried it with me. Over a period of two weeks, I began to gather evidence about what I was *already* doing that promoted that Life's Intention. That was a change, right there! For example, I was already drinking the amount of water suggested for good physical health. My guilt — that feeling that's always there when I concentrate on losing weight — decreased substantially with this new focus. From that foundation, I began to find ways to demonstrate that Life's Intention with a little more ease and grace. I'd ask myself in various situations, 'How would a person who is willing to be physically fit and healthy act right now?' I developed a goal to walk a fund-raising 5K with two girlfriends. I exercised more to prepare for it and naturally began to eat in a more healthy fashion. Bottom line: here I am after losing fifteen pounds that I've kept off for eight months. I know I've also gained some muscle mass because I've been exercising for my next goal: to cross-country ski with friends around Lake Tahoe this winter. I'm not concentrating on my weight but upon my Life's Intention and a goal worth playing for."

The Brain Is More Malleable Than We Think

As wild as it sounds, you have control over the architecture of your brain. Up until about a decade ago, neurophysiologists thought that past a certain age, the brain stopped producing synaptic connections. The prevalent thought was that there was no way to modify or enrich our brain as we grew older. Recent research has shown that this is simply not true. Because of this, many programs have been developed to help Baby Boomers and others exercise their brains much the same way they exercise their bodies.

At the same time, we are beginning to realize that recurring thoughts produce groovelike synaptic pathways. Think about it like cows on a cow path. Once they begin to carve out a trail across a meadow, other cows follow behind. The road becomes well traveled. You could call it the path of least resistance because it is there, beckoning the next animal forward.

We know that many incidents in life — traumas as well as triumphs — produce these grooved synaptic pathways. We are also beginning to recognize methods, such as eye movement desensitization and reprocessing (EMDR), that can help interrupt the synaptic sequences and provide stressed-out individuals with relief.

So our brains are more malleable and flexible than we previously thought. This is important to know as you learn to shift

the focus of your attention to conclusions that are interesting —
conclusions that really matter to you. You will eventually develop new pathways, and you will notice a subtle shift in the
way you are thinking your thoughts. That is, you may find that
you're not taking yourself quite as seriously as you did in the
past. The notions, situations, behaviors, or issues that used to
tweak you simply don't anymore. The same old thoughts don't
cycle through your head as much. When they do occur, they
have lost the impelling emotional quality they held before. The
"cows" will be taking a different route!

We now have a neurophysiological basis for the metaphysical statement "Thoughts held in mind produce after their
kind." This does not necessarily mean that our thoughts literally create physical reality. Rather, the conclusions we focus
upon automatically guide us to gather evidence to support
them. Evidence to the contrary will be automatically screened
out. For someone who is interested in focusing upon the conclusion that people can be jerks, there will always be compelling
evidence for this. This is what he or she will "see."

By the same token, the phrase "What you focus upon ex-
pands" can have new meaning for us. There's no mystery here.
The good news is that I affect what captures my interest. The
question for all of us is this: What conclusions do I want to base
my life upon? How do I wish to be known?

By now you may see that you can be the expert when it
comes to knowing what is important to you. This knowledge,
combined with the tools we're discussing, will bring you success in playing your games worth playing and goals worth playing for.

STEP THREE

~

Enjoying Ease

CHAPTER EIGHT

What Are You Looking At?

Shifting your attention focuses your efforts with ease, not struggle.

You must first be the change you wish to see in others.

— Mahatma Gandhi

Would you prefer to be known for

- Your complaints or your contributions?

- Your issues or your ideas?

- Your drama or your dreams?

- Your reasons or your results?

Other people know us by how we show up. And, as we've seen, how we show up in life is a function of our conclusions. Our conclusions shape our personal life experiences.

This may sound too simple, and indeed, even as I write it I wonder (or is it my Monkey Mind?) if I shouldn't come up with something deeper and more complex, something harder to grasp and execute. Then it hits me: this lesson isn't filled with struggle and angst because what we're learning here is *ease*.

Look back at the questions above. I suspect you'll notice a difference in your sense of possibility and promise as you look at each of the paired choices. As you look at this difference, ask yourself which side of the equation interests you more.

You might quickly answer, "Of course, the second of each pair is for me." But look closely. For many of us even thinking about this puts us on unfamiliar ground.

Take Esther, for example. She's a colleague of mine. Her eyes sparkle when she talks, and sometimes you don't know if she means what she's saying or is just kidding. But somehow I think she means it when she tells me the following about the choices we just considered: "I'm so used to defining myself in terms of the first side — the issues, drama, and so forth. I'm afraid I'll lose a part of me if I no longer bring those up in conversation. How will I talk about myself? My sisters and I always get together to discuss our latest issues with work or people in our lives. It sounds silly, but if I don't complain or go into my drama, what will I have to say? What will I have if let this stuff go?"

Monkey Mind shows up twitching its tail when we contemplate a shift in our state of being. And this is precisely what happens when we take the focus of our attention off who we are psychologically (our thoughts and feelings, issues and dramas) and put it upon who we are ontologically (our unchanging, essential nature). Monkey Mind stands at the portal and begs us to turn back.

"Let's face it," says this part of our mind. "All those memories of past failures are painful, yes. But at least the pain is familiar." In other words, this banana tree may have no more fruit on it, but at least it is a well-known tree. Fear of the unknown is strong. Even ease, in its unfamiliarity, can make us, well, uneasy. This is important to acknowledge — and observe — but it needn't prevent us from pursuing the path toward luminosity.

Ontological Conclusions Lead to Luminous Experiences

That said, remember that you now have two methods for shifting the focus of your attention from one set of conclusions to another:

* Developing the capacity to observe rather than analyze

* Seeing that it is possible to be willing, no matter what you think or feel

You also have two categories of ontological conclusions on which you may choose to focus:

* Your Life's Intentions

* Your Standards of Integrity

We are now going to put these all together to create luminous experiences. Let's begin by becoming even clearer about what we mean by *ontology*. Let's give the word vigor and presence. When you see into your ontological nature, you'll have the capacity to bring that aspect of yourself to bear upon everyday situations. And that's where luminosity lives — not in the rarified atmosphere of metaphysical reality, but in the actions you take at work, in your community, and with those you love.

To recap just a bit, your Life's Intentions and Standards of Integrity are your internal anchors. They belong to you, no matter what you think or feel at any moment. In other words, your Life's Intentions and Standards of Integrity are not affected in the least by anything that goes on in your head. They speak to an aspect of you that transcends intellect and emotion. They reflect your personal brilliance. When you take action in accord with them, you are led to luminosity.

This is because who we truly are — at the heart of our being — is bigger than our thoughts, feelings, diagnoses, and labels. While we can't see directly into this heart of being, we can observe its reflection, one example of which is our Standards of Integrity. Like the Caribbean fish in chapter 2, who "saw" water for the first time, once you observe something, the knowledge of it is with you for life. You can't "unobserve" it. I have heard from many people that the power and energy of seeing their Standards of Integrity for the first time stays with them forever.

It's Not Psychology versus Ontology

This is not to say you can get rid of who you are psychologically. You wouldn't want to, since your thoughts and feelings, desires and points of view, as well as body sensations make up the richness of your experience.

In fact, the road to luminosity is not without thoughts and feelings that are uncomfortable, even dark. You and I, and all others on this planet, are capable of ideas and opinions that are definitely *not* enlightened.

So we live with a busy brain. It is constantly thinking and feeling. When we don't question what this brain produces — when we don't observe what it is doing — we may not discover that some thoughts are worth thinking and others aren't. As you wake up and clear away the fog, something paradoxical happens. You come to see even more of the contents of your mind. And sometimes those contents don't look so good. To be conscious, we must be present to everything, the light as well as the dark. You can't choose to wake up just to the stuff you like. But this does not leave us at the mercy of our psychology; we can learn not to be controlled by it.

Here's an example of what I mean. I remember hearing Michael Toms of *New Dimensions Radio* interview Ram Dass, who is arguably one of the great philosophical leaders of our time.[1] Let me paraphrase what I heard. Michael was talking with Ram Dass about his spiritual path and what a gift his teachings were. At one point he asked Ram Dass what the difference was between how he is now and how he was when he was known as Richard Alpert. (Many years ago Richard Alpert and Timothy Leary developed the clinical use of LSD.)

Ram Dass's answer surprised me at first. He said that there was virtually no difference between how he is now and how he was as Richard Alpert. He still has, he explained, the same reactions he always had — being impatient, for example, while waiting in line at a movie theater. The difference is that these feelings don't last as long. I could tell that he'd discovered how not to be controlled by the unpleasant feeling but to instead observe it and then shift his focus of attention to something else, something less aggravating, something of more fundamental interest to him.

That's the trick. And it really is no trick; it's a skill you can hone with practice. As we've discussed, it's all about learning to focus upon the conclusions that matter to you. Focus upon ontological conclusions, such as your Life's Intentions and Standards of Integrity. Put your focus there, and a sense of possibility and promise, a spaciousness and a relaxing around your heart, will follow naturally, *with ease*. No wasted energy —

nothing to struggle with or against. This is how you determine your own psychological experience. We can't control what thoughts and feelings we have; we must observe all of them. But we do have the ability to then shift the focus of our attention to the conclusions that interest us more, letting *those* conclusions generate our experience.

Unlike the process of obsessing about or analyzing our thoughts and feelings, this process — observing and shifting — transforms your life in a gentle, natural way. You live with ease instead of struggle. In other words, luminosity.

Another way to grasp this is to think of a beautifully woven Indian basket. It is spacious. As you look inside, you see a variety of fruits. Some are bright and smell sweet. Some look either unripe or smell bitter. You look inside and, observing all of them, pick the ones you wish to eat. The not-so-appealing fruit is still there, *but you don't have to pick it up*.

Your ontological self is a bit like that basket. It's that aspect of you that witnesses and contains all the fruits of your life. You bring it forth every time you:

- Begin to observe, rather than analyze, what's going on within and around you, including your Monkey Mind symptoms, if they are present.

- Become willing to proceed, no matter what Monkey Mind says.

- Listen instead to your gentle voice of wisdom.

- Focus on your Standards of Integrity and how to put them into physical reality.

- Focus on your Life's Intentions and how to put them into physical reality.

Ontological Questions

One of the best ways to shift the focus of your attention is to ask yourself a question. Questions are informed by conclusions. As we'll see in a moment, there's a difference between questions that originate from a psychological point of view and those that reflect the ontological outlook. Here are some examples of each.

PSYCHOLOGICAL AND ONTOLOGICAL QUESTIONS COMPARED	
PSYCHOLOGY	ONTOLOGY
1. What are my worries, doubts, fears, and concerns?	What really matters to me in life?
2. Why is this happening? Why am I feeling this way?	How might what I'm going through contribute to the lives of others?
3. What is my history?	What am I grateful for, right here and now?
4. What are the dynamics — motives, family patterns — affecting me?	What are my lessons? How will they help me grow?
5. What should I work on?	What is here for me to explore?
6. Do I really need help? Shouldn't I learn to do this on my own?	Am I inviting and allowing others to support me?
7. How can I get my needs met?	What might I do to benefit the whole?
8. Where have I stopped myself? Why have I done this?	What is a game worth playing and goals worth playing for?
9. What needs to be fixed here?	What needs to emerge here?

PSYCHOLOGICAL AND ONTOLOGICAL QUESTIONS COMPARED (*Continued*)	
PSYCHOLOGY	ONTOLOGY
10. How can I become more comfortable?	How might I wake up and lift the fog?
11. How might I do the things I need to do quickly and efficiently?	How might I do what's before me with clarity, focus, ease, and grace?
12. What do I want to do?	What am I willing to do?

These are just some examples of questions arising from two different sets of conclusions. Look at the first column. If you're like most of us, it sounds familiar. These are questions that produce answers without an ontological container. The answers to those questions don't take us anywhere new.

As you look at the ontological questions, it's obvious that thoughts and feelings are associated with them. Once again, it's impossible to divorce yourself from who you are psychologically. However, these thoughts and feelings have a different quality. There is possibility, promise, a sense that all is well. You might notice a smile emerge as you read the ontological questions. Or you might find your heart relaxing. The questions carry a different energy, a path to luminosity paved with ease.

These ontological questions also elicit your natural wisdom and ability. Think for a moment about your mentors or guides, people who have done what you consider to be admirable. I'll bet that they focused upon one or more of the above ontological questions or close versions of them. The questions we ask ourselves shape our lives. The most powerful ones open us to possibility. Others lead to more fog.

I suggest you refer to these questions later on when we look more closely at your personal games worth playing and goals worth playing for. These questions are designed to help you get past the Trouble at the Border we all experience when bringing an idea from metaphysical to physical reality. These questions are a valuable part of your tool kit.

Seeing Others through Ontological Lenses

Let's now take what we've learned about conclusions a step further. If luminosity is reached through demonstrating who we are ontologically, then in order to generate luminous experiences, we must develop the capacity to gather ontological evidence about *other* people as well.

Recall the "my boss is a jerk" scenario. There's no way around it: how I show up in the face of that evidence is small-minded and defensive, my heart closed. I want to avoid him, not so much because of him, but because of how I feel and act when I'm around him. Juxtapose my conclusion about my boss with the conclusions we explored Mother Teresa as having.

You might be tempted to think that Mother Teresa never had "unenlightened" thoughts about other people. You'd be mistaken. She had keen self-awareness. And profound self-awareness turns up more than sunshine and light. In his book *The Mystic Heart*, Wayne Teasdale writes that Mother Teresa was interviewed about the early days of starting her mission. The interviewer wanted to know how she was able to work with people who were dying, poor, and abandoned. To show him the range of her motivations, she related a time when she was a young woman and had a disturbing insight about herself. In addition to her generous nature, she related that "I realized a long time ago that I had a Hitler within me."[2]

That startled me. I had always supposed that those whom I consider to be saints and wise people never had really negative thoughts, as I do. How often are we glad that people can't read our minds because we ourselves are unhappy about the thoughts we have? But when you are aware of all the different kinds of thoughts you have about people — the generous and the not so generous — and when you tell the truth to yourself about it, you gain some breathing room. You are then able to shift the focus of your attention to the conclusions about others that interest you the most. And your personal pathway to luminosity depends upon your ability to see the hero in other people. Luminosity isn't a one-way street. You learn to focus on your own ontological qualities, and you learn to focus on the ontological qualities of other people as well.

Think of it this way: when you live in a smoggy city, you sometimes don't even see the smog. There are some days in Los Angeles, for example, when the sky may appear clear and blue. But if you hop on a plane and look out your window at around seven thousand feet, you'll see a brown haze. What you thought was a clear day really wasn't. The smog was there all along, but you had gotten so used to it you didn't notice it.

Smog dulls colors and masks the smells of the seasons. The world looks slightly gray. Even when smog doesn't burn your eyes, your body may still react to it — your breathing may get shallower and you may feel tired without knowing why. Flying above the smog, you see the vivid blue sky and bright white clouds. This always relaxes and invigorates me. I feel I'm seeing the colors the way they were meant to be seen.

A fresh perspective gives you a lift, like flying above the smog. You see that your vision may not have been as clear and comprehensive as you thought it was. We want to see other people in a way that is vibrant and clear, in the way they were meant to be seen.

To understand this more deeply, let's compare and contrast two different ways of looking at people. Find a photo of someone you care about. If you don't have one near at hand, then simply picture this person in your mind. As you read the following, imagine this person in front of you so that you can get a direct experience of what we're talking about.

If you held the first, psychological perspective, you could entertain at least six different conclusions about this person. You could gather evidence for the following:

- This person is damaged in some way and needs to be fixed. There is something wrong with him — maybe not everything, but *something*.

- This person does not have her own answers. She's clueless about some aspect of her life. Not only is she driving in the fog, but even if the fog were to lift, she *still* wouldn't know what to do.

- I have the answers for this person, and it's up to me to fix him or give him good advice.

- This person doesn't have many goals or dreams worth playing for.

- I question this person's commitment, motivation, and ability.

- I feel that this person is a drain on me, taking up my energy or time.

Notice your experience as you apply one or more of those six conclusions to the person you're focused upon. I realize this is an artificial situation and it may be difficult, but try it anyway. How would you begin to act around this person? Is there any room for possibility, creativity, collaboration, or support? Does your heart constrict somewhat? Note the reactions for yourself. We all have our own reactions when we view people through one or more of the above conclusions. The point is to get in touch with your own version of the smog that rolls in when you see people in this way.

Richard talked with me about his reaction to seeing his students in this way. He's a forty-two-year-old junior college biology professor. His green eyes are usually bright, but today as he talks to me about what concerns him, his handsome face has become a mask of tension. The smile fades. His voice becomes a monotone. "Sometimes I don't even know if I should continue with this teaching job. I'm getting too irritated with the students. For instance, there's this one guy, Allen. He says he wants to be a physical therapist, but he's always late to class. Has a great excuse every time. I don't think he's really motivated or else he'd make this class a priority. He's not taking his education seriously enough. And that's what it's like for fifty percent of the students I teach. It's like pulling teeth to get them to think for themselves. And to top it off, they complain every time I give them homework. Like I said, maybe I'm just in the wrong field."

I remember earlier that week asking Richard about how his teaching was going. His response was, "Well, it's the same ol' same ol'." Phrases like this are good smog indicators.

I know Richard. One of his Life's Intentions is to be an effective teacher, and he cares about his students. Nevertheless, anyone in his shoes could come to see his students the same way. Richard could probably get plenty of empathy from fellow faculty. It's normal to think the way he does. And that's the problem because what's "normal" isn't going to bring him — or us — closer to luminosity.

Normal refers to what's typical, customary, or usual. The sorts of conclusions we've listed above are, unfortunately, normal. They're our path of least resistance, our default setting, what we're familiar with. Whether we're referring to friends, colleagues, loved ones, or fellow employees, we can gather huge dossiers full of evidence to support these conclusions. They form the basis of our common conversations. In my experience with thousands of people over the years — in board meetings, hospital staff conferences, community assemblies, professional committees, and chats between friends — I've noticed we are drawn toward conclusions of this nature like bees to honey.

It would have been "normal" for Mother Teresa to view the people she served in Calcutta through the conclusions listed above. But she didn't. What she saw in people was extraordinary. And we can learn to emulate it.

Now let's look at six other conclusions you could entertain about the person whose photo is in front of you or whose face is in your mind right now. You could gather evidence for the following:

- This person is a hero, whole and complete just the way she is.

- This person has goals and dreams and a desire to make a difference.

- This person has loved ones — people he loves and who love him.

- This person has Standards of Integrity and Life's Intentions, whether or not she knows at this time what they are.

- This person makes a contribution to me in some way.

- This person is worthy of being treated with dignity and respect in the way I interact with him.

Notice the shift in your energy as you apply one or more of these conclusions to the person upon whom you're focused. You might notice your body relaxing and a sense that all is well. When I apply these conclusions, I also feel a sense of ease; I don't need to analyze or fix or change this person. A burden is lifted, and luminosity draws nearer.

Practice seeing people according to this second perspective, and you are opening your heart of compassion. There is spaciousness and possibility here. You have adopted the ontological view. It is the result of seeing directly into the heart of who people really are. This is the way they — and you — are meant to be seen.

Think for a moment of the conversations you could have with anyone if this were the way you saw them. Would more clarity, focus, ease, and grace be present? Extend this to the people with whom you work. What kinds of staff meetings could take place if you saw people in the manner above?

It is tremendously supportive to be in the presence of someone who sees you through the lens of these conclusions. They see beyond — or above — the smog of your transitory thoughts, feelings, and behaviors. They know that you are more than those, bigger than them. Even if you have behaved badly — *especially* if you have behaved badly — these mentors, friends, family members, ministers, or coaches still see the best in you. And because they do, you are empowered. The fog — or smog — of your thoughts and feelings lifts. You are put back in touch with your essential nature because *they* have not lost sight of it.

Adopting the ontological view takes courage. It is bucking the normal way of seeing people. But think about the difference it would make if you were to copy the above conclusions on a three-by-five card and take them with you into staff meetings, client conferences, family get-togethers, or the classroom. What if you tried seeing everyone like this, no matter what they did?

As you think about this, your Monkey Mind might start saying something like, "Don't do it! Pay no attention to this exercise! Back away from those conclusions and no one will get hurt!" You — and your Monkey Mind — might have a lot to say at this point.

Disregard what people do? Ignore bad behavior? No. This is not what I'm suggesting. I'm instead focusing on *you* — on giving you tools and helping you improve your life no matter what "they" do. Nod in acknowledgment of Monkey Mind's protective impulses, but nevertheless turn your attention toward a new way of seeing.

We're expanding your skill set for success. Remember, success is doing what you said you would do with clarity, focus, ease, and grace. It requires a reorientation, within and without, to the ontological view. If you take out your Life's Intentions list and your Standards of Integrity card and lay them next to those ontological conclusions listed above, you have new tools for creating a life filled with luminous experiences. Not only do you see your own basic goodness, but you also are beginning to see the same in others. After all, those ontological conclusions simply indicate that others have Standards of Integrity and Life's Intentions, just as you do. We are acknowledging the light and the dark (Mother Teresa's "Hitler") in ourselves and in others. And in the face of this acknowledgment we are nevertheless willing to shift toward the light. How masterful is that?

Another View — Meditation

A brief exploration of meditation is helpful here. There are many kinds of meditation. In one form you close your eyes and watch your thoughts, shifting the focus of your attention away from usual thoughts and toward the object of your desire, whether a mantra or a spiritual saying. Every time you notice that you are going back to your customary thoughts, you observe that this is so and redirect your attention.

What if we were to consider that life is really an eyes-open meditation? Whether we're alone, with friends, or at work, we have the choice to observe the nature of our thoughts and then shift the focus of our attention to thoughts worth thinking and conclusions worth gathering evidence for. Our experience of life, our degree of discomfort or ease, is governed by our focus. Where we put our attention gives us our evidence. In this way we can see that what governs our experience in life is not necessarily our outward circumstances. Instead, it's what we say about these circumstances.

Try the following:

- Copy down the ontological conclusions about others *
  that we outlined earlier in this chapter onto a three-by-
  five card.

- Take this card with you to a meeting or interaction,
  whether at work, in your community, at church, or at
  home.

- If you find a difficult situation brewing — something
  not going as planned — take out the card for a moment.
  (Of course this might have to be on the sly since others
  might not know what you're doing.)

- Look at the qualities you listed on the card.

- Ask yourself the following: How might this interaction
  turn out if I were to see this person in terms of these
  qualities?

- Don't force yourself to see anything about them. Keep
  your focus gentle. Just a moment of considering these
  qualities can often produce a breakthrough in what
  happens between you.

- Even if you see few or no results, acknowledge yourself
  for being willing to try this. Just being willing to do
  this often gives you new breathing room.

The key to shifting the focus of your attention is being gentle
with yourself. Some thoughts and conclusions have been
around us for so long that they've taken up residence in the living room of our minds. They've got their feet up and are quite
comfortable just where they are. Even the discomfort they
prompt is comfortable in the sense that it is familiar; it feels

safe. However, simply turning your focus to ontological conclusions, even for only a few minutes a day, will give them the
idea that they are no longer as welcome as they were in the past.
Without you having to boot them out the door — with ease
rather than drama and struggle — they'll get the idea and move
out of your way.

CHAPTER NINE

Energy Efficiency

*You can direct the energies of money, time, physical vitality,
creativity, enjoyment, and relationship.*

*By recording your dreams and goals on paper, you set in mo-
tion the process of becoming the person you most want to be.
Put your future in good hands — your own.*

— Mark Victor Hansen

Having read this far, you are probably raring to go. You want
to get started on a goal. What do you do next? If you direct
your energy — all your energies — properly, the goal will take
shape with ease. Here's a real-life example.

Sue is singing. In front of more than a hundred friends and
family, at a community center in her neighborhood, she's having her first ever voice recital. She's wearing a dress she made
especially for the occasion, a floor-length gown in a blue floral
pattern with a matching scarf that she holds in her hand, letting
one end trail down, like an opera diva. At the conclusion, her
husband of forty years walks down the middle aisle with two

dozen long-stemmed red roses. He gives her a big smooch, and we get it all on videotape.

How Sue got to this point is the clearest demonstration I know of using the principles we've been exploring.

It had begun ten months earlier, in something Sue said during my seminar: "I'm sixty-two now. I've wanted to have a voice recital — just me alone with a piano, in front of friends — for forty years now. When I was twenty-two I talked myself out of it because I had just gotten married and my husband needed me on the farm. Then I had kids, and at thirty-two I decided to wait until they were out of high school before I pursued this dream. Then at forty-two, it was because my firstborn was getting married. It was always something. I can understand putting a dream off for a while. But forty years?"

Sue had just taken the Life's Intentions Inventory. "To be an adventurer" scored a 5. And the voice recital was an adventure for sure, one that she wasn't going to put off any longer. This was a game worth playing and a goal worth playing for.

To meet her goal, Sue needed to learn to use six kinds of energy. If you're going to have what you truly want in life with clarity, focus, ease, and grace, you too need to focus these six energies toward your goals. The six energies are: money, time, physical vitality, creativity, enjoyment, and relationship.

This is how they worked for Sue. She focused her:

- Money — to get voice lessons, hire a piano accompanist, and rent the community center room.

- Time — because although she had a great voice and

had sung light opera as a young woman, she needed to practice.

- Physical vitality — "You have no idea how much energy it takes to learn to sing loudly. I had to strengthen my diaphragm, and it's harder than you think."

- Creativity — in making that floor-length dress with matching scarf.

- Enjoyment — she kept a journal of the experience that let her savor every moment of the journey.

- Relationships — she let her friends cheer her on. In fact, twelve of us decided to form a "ladies' tea-pouring society" for the event. We found white gloves and served tea and cookies to everyone who showed up. In addition, for the month before her recital, one of us called her every day to see how she was doing.

The day of the event, as Sue sang, a transformation took place right before us. She became that twenty-two-year-old again. You could see it in her eyes and hear it in the vitality of her voice. That young woman who had put her dream off for forty years was back!

The moment was luminous for everyone. Even as I write this now, I can see the whole scene, though it took place over fifteen years ago. Sue caught the fire of engagement with life. She decided to travel around the world once each year to sing at sacred sites. The first was a place called Taizé, in France. The postcards I received were vivid and filled with tidbits about the people she was meeting and the adventures she embraced.

Becoming a Conscious Conduit of Energy

You and I are here to become conscious conduits of energy, as we just read about Sue doing. A conduit is like a channel. It's a way to organize energy so that it can do something in physical reality and not get wasted. Think of it this way: you have a clear blue pond of cool water. Twenty yards away, you have a flower garden you want to nourish. The question becomes how to get the water from the pond to that garden.

This may seem simple, but in the way we use energy in our lives, we don't act as though this is obvious. The density of physical reality requires that we master our use of energy so we can attain what really matters to us — so we have a shot at luminosity. A dead garden is not luminous.

We get a pipe to conduct energy from the pond to the garden. And here we begin to discover a principle for success. Energy requires a conduit to do work in physical reality. Energy without a conduit lies unused and dormant. It dissipates or stagnates. It can't be focused in order to be of benefit.

In ancient times people learned to make conduits to direct water. It changed human life. Before discovering how to make furrows to carry water, people collected food and were at the mercy of rivers or lakes, which would overflow or recede. But with a conduit for water, agriculture began. People no longer had to wander across the plains hunting and gathering. Instead, many settled down and created towns, where different forms of culture developed.

Not only does energy require a conduit, but at the same time, a conduit must have energy to do its job. This is another success principle. Without energy moving through it, a conduit becomes empty and useless.

You are that conduit we're talking about. You are perfectly designed to have energy move through you so that you can nurture your garden of goals and dreams.

Energy has to be directed. When the pipe is drawing water from the lake, we want to make sure it's pointed in the right direction. You can have abundant energy pouring through that pipe, but if it isn't aimed at the garden, the flowers will still wither and die. We see this analogy in how we use our own energy. For example, we may have all the energy we need in the shape of time, money, and physical vitality to create and live in luminous moments, but we still need to learn to direct this energy in an astute and discerning way toward the ideas and dreams we wish to nourish and grow.

In addition, to work well, a conduit can't have sediment and sludge. Energy has to flow unobstructed, with ease. Now, it's normal in physical reality to come across a pipe that is plugged up with sediment. As it pertains to you, we will define *sludge* as the incomplete use of your life's energy. This is about unfinished business, which can cause you to fail to achieve what you truly want. It's not comfortable to look at this. However, if you are willing to do it anyway, I promise that you will experience greater clarity, focus, ease, and grace as you play the games you were meant to play. In other words, you will be a conscious conduit of energy.

To be successful, a conduit can't have leaks. Whether it's a water pipe, a levee, or an electric wire, years of use can wear down places where energy then escapes. For our purposes, you know you're leaking energy when:

- You're not getting true satisfaction from using it.
- You're not doing anything with it that is of value or benefit to you, your community, or those you love.

- You have a sense that you "don't know where it's gone."

Incidentally, we already have an intuitive sense that time, money, physical vitality, creativity, enjoyment, and relationship are forms of energy. Look at the words we use. For instance, when we speak of using energy effectively, we talk about investing it, spending it, and conserving it. When we describe the ineffective use of energy, we speak of wasting it, losing it, or squandering it. You have probably used those words to describe your relationship with money, time, and physical vitality. As we go along, you'll find that the same metaphors hold true for the energies of creativity, enjoyment, and relationship as well.

In this chapter we will go over each kind of energy and what it takes to direct it so that it flows with ease. We'll see examples of the effective and ineffective use of this energy. Just as Sue did, you can experience the thrill of achieving the goals that are waiting for you with your name written all over them.

Each of us has a different relationship with these six forms of energy. For some, money is what we need to learn to direct. For others, time is what we're here to master. For others, lessons about physical vitality and support present the greatest opportunities for growth. At the same time, all the forms of energy are connected, which means that how you relate to one gives you clues about how you relate to all of them. As you look at the following examples, see what's true for you.

The Energy of Money

My journey toward effective use of energy began with my own unconsciousness about the energy of money. Many years ago, listening to my Monkey Mind, I made some unwise business decisions that cost me thousands of dollars. I so wanted to blame others for these failures! After a while I began to blame myself. Both strategies brought in the fog. It was obvious I had to learn to observe where I was going so that I no longer ran into those oncoming trucks.

If you want to know how the wake-up call regarding money works, you can read about it in *The Energy of Money*. In that book you are guided to thoroughly examine your relationship with that form of energy and are given strategies designed to increase your power to focus it on what you truly want in life.

Joseph Campbell said, "Money is congealed energy."[1] *Congealed* means that it's solid; you can hold it in your hands and do something with it. Admittedly, money is a less tangible commodity now that we have credit and debit cards and the means to transfer huge sums of money with the click of a computer key. In fact, in working for twenty-five years with people and their relationship with money, I see that one of the effects of reducing money to an electronic blip is that we relate to it as an abstraction; it's less concrete and solid. We don't get a sense of really spending it until we tally at the end of the month and discover how much of it we actually used. If you want to see what I mean, for the next week pay for everything with cash. Notice how this simple act shifts your experience of money. For instance, you may notice you are spending less of it or that you are more deliberate about what you do buy. There's nothing like pulling $83.59 in paper and coins out of your wallet to make you think about that purchase.

To see money as simply energy divests it of much of the

baggage attached to it through years of psychological probing and self-analysis. It puts money on a par with, say, electricity, which can illuminate a room or give us a nasty shock. The energy is harmful or beneficial depending on how it is used. The same is true for the energy of money. For example, money is neither spiritual nor nonspiritual, good nor bad. This comes as a relief to many who, for much of their professional lives, have undercharged their clients in accord with one or both of the following viewpoints:

- Money isn't spiritual, so if I am in a healing profession and charge money for my services — or charge the fair market rate for them — I'm going against spiritual principles.

- I shouldn't charge money for what I am doing if I am having fun doing it. (A professional organizer I once knew found it hard to charge for her services because she had a ball doing what she did.)

One of the best ways to wake up and become conscious of how you are using the energy of money is to first create a game worth playing and a goal worth playing for. That's because a game and a goal provide structure and an opportunity to begin focusing on how you are using money. Let me show you what I mean as we look at Megan's story.

Megan is an administrative assistant at an advertising firm in San Francisco. At twenty-eight, she's bright and energetic, and you know that she's going places in life. But as she talks to me, it's clear that regarding her vacation plans, she's not going anywhere right now.

"One of my Life's Intentions is to be well traveled. It's unrealistic. I haven't had a good vacation in five years. Maybe that's because I think I don't deserve one or because my parents never took a vacation in all the time I can remember. But it's frustrating. I look at everyone else who's having fun, and I ask myself, What's wrong with this picture?"

Look closely at what she's saying, and I'll bet you can spot at least two or three good Monkey Mind symptoms here. Rationalizations, excuses, comparing herself to others — Monkey Mind has its way with us when we're not taking action toward something that is important to us.

This is what Megan and I did together. She designed a goal, which was to have a one-week Caribbean vacation within a year. So the game looked like this:

Intention: To be well traveled.

Goal: I go on a one-week Caribbean vacation by July 18,
2002 (a year to the day from now).

Time wasn't Megan's problem, money was. She didn't have it and didn't think she would have it in one year's time. I asked her if she was nevertheless *willing*, and she said yes.

In addition, two of Megan's Standards of Integrity were *creative* and *lighthearted*. I asked her if she was willing to play her game in a creative and lighthearted way. Again she said yes.

Having our ontological bases covered, we next looked at where she might be leaking the energy of money. Remember that leaking energy is when you don't get satisfaction or value from the way you're using it. Megan agreed to keep track of every penny she spent for thirty days, not as a budget but to see where the energy was going.

At the end of that period, I got a phone call from her: "I

just finished tracking where I put my money energy. You'll never believe this! I spend at least $7 a day on cappuccino and croissants or other snacks. Seven dollars times at least 220 working days a year is $1540 after-tax income! This has nothing to do with what I do or don't deserve. I'm eating and drinking my vacation away at $7 a pop!"

Megan decided to do something creative and lighthearted about this situation. She promised herself her usual treats on Mondays and Thursdays. This paradoxically increased her sense of enjoyment because that cappuccino and croissant two days a week were now special, something for her to savor. The purchase wasn't a knee-jerk response. The other three days a week she put that same $7 into a vacation savings account. The result? I got a postcard from the Grand Caymans one year later. It was Megan having the time of her life — on a fully paid-for vacation!

Nothing directs the energy of money like having a goal. You begin to weigh momentary spending against a bigger and far more exciting outcome. I've seen people who were sure they had no control over their spending suddenly wake up and begin making very different choices — with ease. All it takes is look-ing at what's important, like your Life's Intentions, and then creating the opportunity to make those intentions a reality. Up goes consciousness, and down goes leaking.

If you are interested in clearing the fog about money from your hero's path, do what Megan did for thirty days. Keep track of what you are spending. Don't deprive yourself. Don't put yourself on a money diet. (When you do that you set up the feast-or-famine pattern that automatically leads to bingeing with money). Simply observe what you do with money, and then ask yourself if it would be all right to use the energy of money more efficiently, in ways that benefit you, your family, your community.

The Energy of Time

Time and money are entwined in our culture and in our individual lives. They are the two major reasons people give for not going for their goals and dreams. In fact, although money is a concern for many of us, I've noticed that conversations about the energy of time are increasing dramatically. As we become busier, we measure out our lives in minutes.

Speaking of minutes, you have 1440 of them each day. Everyone who was ever successful, who attained their heart's desires or created luminous moments, had that same 1440 minutes each day. If you're like many of us, your Monkey Mind is going full throttle right now with reasons why *your* situation is different. I remember my friend Jim telling me, "I know, I know, we all have the same number of minutes. But you don't understand. I *really* don't have time. I'm a school assistant principal. I have two kids of my own, six and eight years old. Sure, one of my Life's Intentions is to be a successful artist. But when I say that there are not enough minutes in the day, I mean it. This isn't an excuse."

I'm meeting with Jim because he is interested in having his teachers learn coaching skills in order to work with their students. He's busy. He's got a lot on his plate. We've just started looking at what would create luminous moments for *him*.

As we've seen, there's no arguing with us when we have amassed a dossier full of evidence. The more someone tries to convince us that what we are talking about may not be the case, the more entrenched we become.

With Jim, I asked him to write the number 1440, the number of minutes in a day. Then I asked him to write the number 10. Ten minutes is less than 1 percent of 1440. However, when you do something that brings you satisfaction for ten minutes a day, at the end of one year you'll have done it for sixty hours. Sixty hours is a college course. It's more than a work-week.

The question to Jim was, "What could you do with sixty hours just for yourself?" Jim decided to spend ten minutes every day, from 5:15 to 5:25 P.M., after work and on most week-ends, in his garage creating watercolor paintings. He reasoned that if it took him about five hours to complete one, he would have it in about a month. Later he admitted to going all the way up to fifteen minutes, but I urged him to keep it at this limit for a while.

His first game worth playing in this area looked like this:

Intention: To be a creator of beauty.
Goal: I complete one watercolor painting by May 30 (one
    month from the present date).

I saw Jim two months after this chat. He'd gone ahead and painted two pictures, but there was an even bigger payoff. This is how he put it: "As you see, I did it. I'm continuing with this, and I'll tell you why. It's changed my life. I'm having fun. But what's more important is that my eight-year-old son, Mark, saw me painting about a week into this. He asked if he could do it too. Now, every day, even on most weekends, Mark and I are in that garage for fifteen minutes. And what a sweet time it is, me and my son. His brother, Adam, doesn't have the attention span right now, but he might want to join us one day. And my wife, Ellen, is happy because I'm not so tense. She says she loves to see me smile."

Luminosity on fifteen minutes a day. Not bad!

In addition to spending ten or twenty minutes a day in a new way, you might want to *stop* spending that time in the same old way. Bring awareness to the amount of time you spend playing computer games, watching television, and so forth, each day, week, or year, and watch the fog lift. You see which side of the road you are on, and you intuitively know what to do next.

The Energy of Physical Vitality

Imagine having a relationship with your body that's a partnership, one in which you and your body are operating as a success team so that you can show up for the games worth playing in your life. The following thought experiment should help set the foundation for this to happen.

Imagine you discover that you and your body aren't communicating very well. You seem to bump into each other. In your mind it's an adversarial relationship. So you decide to send you and your body to a couples' counselor.

There you are, sitting next to your body on a couch in the counselor's office. The counselor turns to you and asks you to talk about your complaints when it comes to your body. You expound for a few minutes. Then the counselor turns to your body and asks, "What are your complaints about this person?"

What would your body say about you? If you're like many of us, it could sound like this:

- "She never feeds me right."
- "He never rests me enough."
- "She's always comparing me to someone else."
- "If I get the slightest pimple, he wants to hide me."
- "When she sees me in the mirror, she gets a look of disgust."

If you were in a personal relationship with someone who treated you this way, how long would you want to remain in it? Then why does the body stay around? To get a peek into this, focus for a moment on the following possibility: your body stays with you because it loves you. It has been your partner since the moment you came into physical reality. It is here with you until you leave. All it has ever wanted to do is support you in being successful at the games you find worth playing.

How would you behave toward someone if you knew they loved you that much? Cynthia gave her answer during a seminar retreat I led at a seaside spa in California: "What a change this point of view is! If I thought my body loved me, I'd treat it like my best friend. I'd want to take care of it and give back what it's giving me. No more complaints. No more talking trash about my body. We'd have fun together. Up until now I focused on whether or not I loved my body. I spent a lot of time on that. Now I'll focus on something else instead — that my body loves me."

It's hard to love your body against the backdrop of the same old complaints. Instead, shift your attention from those complaints to the conclusion that your body loves you. Do this, and you transform your relationship with your body forever. Your behavior with your body, how you show up, follows suit — naturally, gently, with ease.

Take this train of thought a bit further. Your body has never worked against you. It has never sabotaged you. It is simply subject to those three factors in physical reality we looked at earlier: density, impermanence, and unpredictability. There is no motivation to work against you in any way here.

Physical vitality is not about being able to bench-press 150 pounds or run a marathon — unless that's a game worth playing for you. Instead, it's about having the sweet, ease-filled energy to show up for what really matters to you. Let's look more at what this means in the next two stories.

Losing weight is not a goal. No, it isn't. Lower those eyebrows as you read further. Losing weight is the *side effect* of going for a goal. In chapter 7 we heard about Jody transforming her relationship with her body. Stan's story is another example.

Stan, at sixty-one, decided he wanted to jog the Dipsea Trail in California. It starts in the town of Mill Valley, climbs thousands of feet up and down through redwood-lined paths, follows streams, snakes above the fog on wind-blown meadows, and finally drops into Stinson Beach and the cold Pacific. All this is done in a little over seven miles.

Stan didn't want to win the Dipsea Trail race; he simply wanted the joy of participating in it. He started training six months before the event. At that point he was a good twenty-five pounds overweight. He had gained and lost those same pounds ten or twelve times. This time Stan shifted the focus of his attention.

As he put it, "My friends thought I was nuts until I told them I'd jog the Dipsea with clarity, focus, ease, and grace. I started slow because my body has gotten very dense over the years. Impermanence, too — you bet! I'm not twenty-five, and my body has really changed in how much I can exert it. But I have a Life's Intention to be physically fit and healthy. Just dieting and walking four times a week wasn't very exhilarating. No one wakes up in the morning and says, 'Yippee, another day to count calories!' I never kept up with it until I got the game worth playing and goal worth playing for."

Stan's game worth playing looked like this:

Intention: To be physically fit and healthy.
Goal: I jog the Dipsea Trail by August 15, 2004.

Stan prepared. His friends caught his enthusiasm, and two other guys trained to go with him. Each one lost weight. Stan lost eighteen pounds and gained muscle. The adventure took hold of him. Today he's in master's level triathlons and having a great time. He says, "All this new activity is fun, but the luminous moment for me came about a year ago. My son Jeff and I were looking at family pictures one afternoon. We found one of me at the Dipsea Trail. He said, 'Dad, I've been wanting to tell you something for a while now. You're my idol. I'm proud of you for doing all this.' That to me was worth it all!"

Even if you don't train for a jogging event, you still need physical vitality for whatever you do. The secret to having it is to get involved with something that captures your imagination and passion. It's the engagement factor we talked about earlier. When you are engaged in a game worth playing, you naturally begin to find ways to take care of the physical "sludge" that has built up over the years.

Fran (not her real name) is sixty-five, and she has diabetes. Anyone with this condition will tell you that it is tricky to get your blood sugar just right. It takes monitoring because sugar levels are like a moving target. Up until now she hasn't done a good job at it, and she's walking into her physician's office, ready for a lecture.

She doesn't get one because as her doctor told me, "I saw the look on Fran's face when I entered the examining room. Remembering the games-worth-playing concept, I decided to take some extra time with her. Just on a whim, I asked her to fill out the Life's Intentions Inventory. At the top of Fran's list was 'To be a loving grandmother.' I asked her what she would be doing as a grandmother if she felt better physically, and she said she always wanted to show her three grandchildren how to plant a garden."

With this goal in mind and her doctor's encouragement, Fran got creative. She took photos of herself and the kids — ages nine, eleven, and twelve — and some pictures of beautiful gardens. She pasted them all on a piece of cardboard with these words: "I teach Ned, Terry, and Christine to plant a garden by June 16, 2006." This focused her attention on a goal four months in the future. She knew what it would take to get in shape for it. Not only did she begin to faithfully monitor her blood sugar levels, she started walking twenty minutes a day to train for the event.

Her doctor reported, "It was a joy to see her progress. I have the picture of Fran, her grandkids, and the garden they planted in my office to show other people. She feels so good now that she continues to walk with friends every day. You know what? *I* feel successful too!"

To transform your relationship with your body, and recalling the Four-Box Model, get a piece of paper and a pen. You are going to spend the next ten minutes writing down evidence for how much your body loves you. Look at what your body has done for you, how it has supported you through thick and thin (pun intended). Make your examples specific and to the point. For instance, I wrote how my body supported me in making that trip down the Grand Canyon and back. If you hear your Monkey Mind chattering about this, wave at it and shift the focus of your attention back to collecting evidence that your body loves you. Put this piece of paper where you can see it for the next ten days.

The Energy of Enjoyment

When you use the energy of enjoyment, you develop the capacity to savor what is before you. You learn to take delight in what you're doing, not rushing through it and onto the next activity. The opposite of *enjoy* is *consume*, which means to guzzle, chomp through, or use up.

For example, I have discovered that one difference between people who are naturally slim and people who have to work at it is that people who are naturally slim tend to enjoy their food while people like me consume our food.

There I was with my friend who is naturally slender. It's 2:30 on a windy afternoon in San Francisco. We've been seeing clients all morning and decide it's time for a little pick-me-up. We go to a restaurant known for its desserts.

We sit down, side by side, and each of us orders a hot fudge sundae with nuts, whipped cream, and a cherry. I get very intent upon watching my server approach me with my dessert. When she sets it before me, I hunker down over it, my arm protecting this dessert from would-be predators.

I guzzle down that sundae. I don't know if it's because I think someone is going to take it away from me; all I know is that at the end of ten minutes my sundae is gone. I push the empty dish away. Ice cream puddles on the table, chocolate fudge smears in the corners of my mouth, and I hear this little voice inside saying, "I can't believe I ate the whole thing."

Meanwhile, my friend is taking these little nummy bites. She's enjoying every morsel. She says, "Do you notice how the dark chocolate mixes with the vanilla bean of this ice cream? And I do think those are freshly roasted almonds. And the whipped cream is real because I can taste the butterfat on the roof of my mouth."

At the end of ten minutes, my friend pushes a half-eaten sundae away. I hear her muttering three words, which I've yet to comprehend when it comes to ice cream: "I've had enough."

That's good for me, you understand, because I get to eat what's left.

As I'm waddling out of this restaurant, I have an epiphany. I notice that I've eaten three times as much as my friend, and I hardly have a memory of the event because I went through it so quickly. I consumed the dessert. She, by contrast, has eaten less but enjoyed it more. She's satisfied and so is less likely to want something sweet again soon. Me? What hot fudge sundae? It was all a blur.

Cultivating enjoyment is developing a skill. It requires that you be willing to shift the focus of your attention from a conclusion known as "Just let me make it through this" to a conclusion called "What might I savor about this moment?" You take your view off an imaginary future and put it on the very real present.

Take the "enjoyment challenge." Try these strategies out, and look at what you discover about how to use this form of energy.

- For the next three days, resolve to taste everything you eat. You may find, as I did, that you're eating less but are more satisfied.

- Before you buy something that you find at the market checkout counter, where many useless items reside, ask yourself the following: Will I really enjoy what I'm about to fling into my basket?

- As you begin to craft and play toward a goal, ask friends and loved ones to ask you each day what, specifically, you are enjoying about the journey.

These are small adjustments. However, they open you to luminosity, which only occurs in the present moment.

The Energy of Relationship

People who are successful — who act with clarity, focus, ease, and grace — have cultivated rich relationships. Such relationships have two main characteristics. One is the giving and receiving of support. We usually know how to give support. The question is, do we know how to receive it?

Most of us share the myth that if we accept support we diminish our own achievements. Somehow help looks like a crutch, even a personal defeat, or we imagine that it is an imposition on others. But if we stick to this line of reasoning, we scrap any possibility for luminosity.

"I did it myself, but I wasn't alone," explained Sandra. She's talking about how her friends helped her start her executive coaching business and continued, "My friends formed a support system for me. I asked them to come over for a pasta dinner. At the table, I outlined my vision for starting this business and told them I'd need support to get past my Monkey Mind. Deborah gave me the name of someone who had a small office to sublet. Rachael told me about this professional mutual support group she joined and invited me to attend since they didn't have someone who represented professional coaching. Judy gave me the name of a local small business owner's club where they look for speakers. The end result was that I got three clients in two weeks."

We all exist in an interdependent system. No matter how we feel about it, we're linked socially, economically, and ecologically, like cells of a giant organism. We are healthiest when all parts of our bodies and society are functioning together. Margaret Wheatley sums it up in this way: "When we seek connection, we restore the world to wholeness. Our seemingly separate lives become meaningful as we discover how truly necessary we are to each other."

When you ask another person to support you, you are actually giving that person a gift. You're being generous because you're allowing him or her to make a significant contribution to your life. By working together, each of you benefits. The other's act of generosity comes full circle when you let that person know the difference she or he has made.

Recall times in which you knew you had a positive effect on someone else's life. It could be the time you sat down with a friend like Sandra and talked her through a business project. Maybe it was the time you became a mentor for a young person who just needed someone's ear.

The second aspect of a rich relationship is that you talk about what is important to you. I don't mean that every interchange with a friend or colleague has to be "deep and meaningful." I'm pointing instead to the opportunity to engage those around you in conversations that matter because you're talking about your goals, dreams, and Life's Intentions. You're not keeping them to yourself. Like Sandra, you're daring to voice what is in your heart of hearts.

The Energy of Creativity

When I ask people what the energy of creativity means to them, I usually hear something like the following:

- I don't have a creative bone in my body.
- I'm more practical than creative.
- I'm no Michelangelo. I'll leave creativity to artists.

But everyone has creative genius. We all have gifts, talents that get unleashed when we're involved in our games worth playing. I'm talking about the particular way we play those games. You saw it in Sue, with her flowing blue gown; with Fran and the visual guide she made to help her remember her grandkids and garden goal; and with Jim, who found a brilliant way to paint pictures in only fifteen minutes a day.

Over the years, I've found we often undervalue our creative abilities because they come so easily to us. We don't realize we are being creative. For example, has anyone ever acknowledged you for something that you do well — like preparing a meal, designing a brochure, or organizing a party — and the first thing you hear yourself saying is, "It's nothing"? Conversely, do you ever look at someone else's talent and compare yourself to them to your own disadvantage?

I've worked with many people who thought they weren't creative because they overlooked their natural aptitude in favor of someone else's ability. It's time to put this all to rest. *You* are resourceful and ingenious.

One secret to creating luminous experiences with ease is to find out what you do well and use those talents as you play toward your goal. You can find out all about your gifts if you're willing to do something that's courageous and, well, creative.

Ask your friends, family, and close colleagues what they have observed that you do well. This is using the energy of relationship to support you. Don't disregard or downplay ("it's nothing") what they say. Give them the pleasure of accepting this gift.

Here are the questions you could ask others that will give you feedback about your creative genius:

- What are three things that you think I do well?

- Think of something you complimented me on in the past and that I made light of. What was it?

- If somebody else asked you to describe two of my talents or skills, what would you list?

No matter what your Monkey Mind says, take notes. Look for anything peeking out between the words. Different people might express the same concept in their own ways. When I did this with my friends and family, one talent they pointed to is my ability to improvise. I never thought of it as anything special since it's something that comes naturally to me. I find creative solutions to problems by finding new ways to deal with obstacles. This happens whether I'm cooking, planning a trip, or dealing with a seminar event in which the audiovisual equipment has stopped working.

Now that it has a name, I have another tool. When confronted by the obstacles that naturally go along with density, impermanence, and unpredictability, I call upon this ability consciously. I ask myself how someone who's brilliant at improvisation would handle this situation. (It works!)

It's Time to Create a Game

Right now, are you willing to pick a game worth playing and goal worth playing for? Remember, luminosity is the result of *action* that reflects who you are.

1. Find a Life's Intention that scored a 5 for you. Write it down.

2. If Monkey Mind starts chattering as you do this, simply say, "Duly noted!" and shift the focus of your attention back to that Life's Intention.

3. Put "I am willing" in front of what you wrote.

4. Now create a goal. It's an area or object toward which play is directed in order to score. It has the following five components; make sure each one is reflected in your goal.

   - *S* is for *specific*: Dollar amount in an investment portfolio, planting a garden, writing a short story, walking a 5K, painting a picture, or giving a voice recital.

   - *M* is for *measurable*: What kind of a garden, what type of short story, where the walk will take place. Measurable is related to specific, but here we get the picture of it in our minds.

- *A* is for *attainable*. We want it to be a small stretch. Remember, this is a practice goal. We want you to lower the bar so that when you reach this goal you won't be too exhausted to enjoy it.

- *R* is for *relevant*. The goal must have meaning for you. That's the whole purpose of engaging in this game. Meaning comes from seeing a Life's Intention being demonstrated by this goal. It also comes from seeing the Standards of Integrity you use while playing for it.

- *T* is for *time based*. Attach a day, month, and year to this goal, the date you'll have reached it. (For your first goal, make it no later than six months from today.)

Keep your description short and to the point. Here are some examples, drawn from the thousands who've done this already, to give you a push in the right direction:

Life's Intention: To be a loving husband.
Goal: Susan and I are on a romantic weekend by June 15, 2007.

Life's Intention: To be spiritually developing.
Goal: I am at a Zen meditation retreat by September 30, 2007.

Life's Intention: To be a successful author.
Goal: My children's book manuscript is complete by November 21, 2007.

Life's Intention: To be physically fit and healthy.
Goal: I bike 50 miles from inn to inn in Vermont by October 25, 2007.

Life's Intention: To be a creator of beauty.

Goal: I plant an herb and flower garden by May 12, 2007.

Your goal moves you from insight to action. Find a game, any game, and we'll go forward. If your Monkey Mind puts up a fuss because you might not have "the right game," simply wave at it and write something down anyway. I promise you'll see that the content of your game matters less than that you step right up and *play*. In fact, what is most important is who you discover yourself to be as you play for that goal.

CHAPTER TEN

It's How You Play the Game

Every successful game has five stages.

*For a long time it had seemed to me that life was about to begin
— real life. But there was always some obstacle in the way —
something to be got through first, some unfinished business,
time still to be served, a debt to be paid. Then life would begin.
At last it dawned on me that these obstacles were my life. This
perspective helped me to see that there is no way to happiness.
Happiness is the way.*

— Fr. Alfred D'Souza

The *Encarta Dictionary* tells us that the word *easy* means re-
quiring little effort, work, or thought. But we also know that
little effort translates into little energy. When something is too
easy for us, we tend to get bored or make mistakes because we
take our eye off what we're doing. Without challenge, we stop
focusing.

I'm not asking you to avoid situations that are easy. We all
need times to just hang out and enjoy ourselves. In fact, one
question I asked you at the beginning of this book was "Would
it be all right with you if life got easier?"

However, the quality we're after here is *ease*, not *easy*. The word *ease* means something different — a quality of action that can lead us toward luminous moments. Some synonyms for *ease* are *naturalness*, *simplicity*, and *straightforwardness*. *Ease* in this sense doesn't imply working without effort. Rather, the effort is focused in a clear direction, and there is no strain. What this means is that you can work hard *with ease*.

The opposite of ease isn't difficulty; the opposite of ease is struggle. Struggle is what we do when we:

- Wait by the side of our hero's path for Monkey Mind to go away before moving forward.

- Analyze, rather than observe, the nature of that Monkey Mind.

- Engage in a lot of activity that has no meaning but that serves as a distraction from our goals and dreams.

- Continue to gather evidence for conclusions that constrict our sense of possibility without getting us one inch closer to those dreams.

We have tools in our kits now to minimize struggle. And we understand that effort is always needed to navigate the passage from metaphysical to physical reality. (Remember Trouble at the Border?) We know that obstacles are part of the game, but as we've been discovering, ease can be part of our game too.

In a moment we are going to explore the five stages that any successful game goes through and what to do at each stage to increase the possibility for ease in your play. But since life doesn't always occur in neat stages and according to plan, we'll first look at what you can do when confronted with, well, a mess.

When Ease Isn't Easy

As many people do, I hold as one of my Life's Intentions "To be a contributor to my community." Focusing on that desire has stopped me from throwing in the towel a number of times when I met physical reality with a loud crunch at the border. I'll give you an illustration that is very vivid for me.

A few years ago I had the privilege of presenting at a conference of the National Institute for the Clinical Application of Behavioral Medicine, held at Hilton Head, South Carolina. It's an honor to be invited to speak to these people. They are in the forefront of the healing profession.

There I am on the morning of my presentation. I've flown in late from California the night before. I'm in the speaker's lounge having oatmeal. I'm mentally preparing for the presentation coming up in about an hour, wanting to make sure that I'm as clear as possible. I'm dressed in my old green sweats and running shoes. No makeup. Hair disheveled. Haven't brushed my teeth yet. But I'm feeling great because I have some time to breathe before I need to get dressed.

Suddenly the doors to the lounge fling open. The coordinator of the conference calls out my name. "Maria," she says, looking alarmed, "you were supposed to be downstairs at your presentation ten minutes ago!"

I had set my watch to the wrong time!

Two words escape my mouth. They start with the letters *o* and *s*. Heart racing, I rush from that room, realizing that there's no time to get dressed. As the elevator descends toward the conference hall, I'm running fingers through my hair to get it to look a little less Einsteinian.

Instead of reviewing my whole life at that moment, as I

would have done some years earlier, I review my Life's Intentions. Since one of them is "To be a contributor to my community," I begin to ask myself how this very situation might contribute to the people I'm about to meet. My heart starts to calm down and open up.

I enter the lecture hall. About two hundred people are there, and they are not very happy because by this point I'm almost twenty minutes late. I'm walking up the center aisle, and they don't know I'm the speaker because of the way I look. The subject of this talk is the hero's journey, including Trouble at the Border. And now I'm living it. I step up onto the stage, and while I'm being fitted with the microphone, I ask them, "Have you ever had a nightmare in which you were supposed to be giving a presentation and you got the wrong time and wound up in front of a big group of people both late and looking terrible?"

There is a pause. Then everyone starts to laugh. I ask them to support me by visualizing the gorgeous black and purple outfit I was going to wear to impress them. We all laugh some more. I launch into a presentation on Trouble at the Border, and we look at what just happened in light of this phenomenon. And I'm passing through the border — with ease — even as I talk about it.

Before I started following the principles in this book, I was confronted at times with similarly messy events. No matter how much you try to prepare, you will always meet up with these unforeseen moments. Back then, my attention automatically went to my mortified self — and stayed there. If the above situation had occurred years ago, I might have suggested to the conference coordinator that she adjourn that session without having me speak. What's more, I would have listened to Monkey Mind for the next week or two — How could I *do* that? What's my problem? I should find another line of work.

But in this scenario, instead of terror and self-recrimination, there was compassion and a gentle good humor. There was the opportunity to be more innovative because I was in the observational rather than analytic mode. One woman even asked me afterward if I'd planned to give my talk in this way. (No!) Fortunately, I had remembered to shift the focus of my attention from my discomfort to a conclusion that was more interesting — the opportunity to contribute. My attention went off me and onto the people I was with. How I showed up followed suit. The result? A moment of luminosity pulled out of the density, impermanence, and unpredictability of physical reality. Whew.

So let's move on to those five stages all games go through. Each phase requires that you use energy differently. And each presents its own pitfalls as well as possibilities.

Although we use the metaphor of a game, you could substitute the word *project*, such as writing a book, starting a business, launching a new product, learning to carry on a twenty-minute conversation in a new language, planning a party for your children, or training for a marathon. The main characteristic here is that your game (project) has a beginning, middle, and end. It isn't a process that continues over a period of time, such as exercising three times a week or answering your email in a timely manner. While those are important, they don't really have end points. In that sense, there's no real goal that you attain and then move on from.

As we've said, you are shaped by the games you play. In the end, you discover that the specific content of any game is not as important as the fact that you are *engaged* with your life. At each point in your game you have the opportunity to play with clarity, focus, ease, and grace. And here the spotlight is on ease.

Stage One: Creation

The first stage of your game, creation, occurs in metaphysical reality. When you have covered the following points, you have built a powerful field on which to play for your goal.

A. BE CLEAR ABOUT YOUR GOAL AND THE LIFE'S INTENTION FUELING IT. One key reason people don't reach their goals is because what they thought was a goal wasn't! In the last chapter we looked at the five qualities your goal needs in order to be a real goal: it needs to be specific, measurable, attainable, relevant, and time based. Only in this way can it serve as a container for the energy that you're going to focus. For example,

- If you aren't *specific* about your goal, you'll never get off the ground with it no matter how much energy you expend.

- Let's say you get specific, as in having a financial portfolio or writing a book, but your goal is not *measurable*, such as six hundred dollars in the portfolio or a book about hiking in the Sierra. How will you know where to focus that energy?

- If the above two conditions are met but your goal isn't *attainable*, you're creating conditions for frustration, as in energy down the drain.

- Similarly, if the goal is attainable but it isn't *relevant* or meaningful because you haven't identified the Life's

Intention behind it, then you'll let go of the goal when you feel physical reality pushing back. It will fly away from you like a helium balloon because it wasn't tethered to something important to you.

• Finally, if all of the above conditions are met, but there's no *time* specified, the whole enterprise could go on forever, taking barrels of energy along with it.

So create a true goal, and you have a container for all of your precious energy.

B. LOOK FOR THE RICH RELATIONSHIPS THAT SURROUND YOU. We are all interconnected. We are stronger when we operate as a network. People who are successful know this in their bones. Right at this moment, you know people who would be honored if you asked for their support in your game. Who knows, this might inspire them to ask for support for their own goals. Find at least two people. When you ask for their assistance, do something that will make their job easier: show them your list of Monkey Mind symptoms, and let them know which ones frequently appear in front of you when you're in Trouble at the Border.

Talk with this support system about the phrases that emerge right before you're about to give up on a goal or dream. Be as specific as possible. You want to give them a success experience in supporting you. You don't want them to cave in to the persuasiveness of your self-limiting internal dialogue. Give them permission to engage with you in conversations designed to identify and observe Monkey Mind symptoms so that you can refocus your attention on the game.

The idea of educating your support system comes from the

movie *Young Frankenstein*. Gene Wilder, as Dr. Frankenstein, is about to enter a dark dungeon to face and "tame" the monster he's just created. He tells Frau Blücher, played by Cloris Leachman, not to let him leave the room, no matter how much he pleads with her to do so, until he accomplishes this task. Sure enough, he goes in, sees the monster, and turns and bangs on the door to be let out. However, Frau Blücher has been prepared. She keeps the door shut. He has no recourse but to turn, face the monster, and strike up a friendship.

You may not expect such a dramatic turn of events, but you still need to educate those who are going to help you past the border and keep you on track while you go for your goal. Remember that allowing someone to support you like this actually gives that person a gift as well.

C. HAVE YOUR STANDARDS OF INTEGRITY NEAR AT HAND. Just as important as playing for the goal itself is declaring the specific qualities or attributes you are willing to bring forth while you're playing. That, along with being specific about your Life's Intention, brings the ontological dimension of the game to the forefront. As you focus on ontological conclusions, you gain access to an aspect of yourself that is timeless and that transcends your psychological doubts and worries.

D. REMEMBER TO BE WILLING. Being willing is the capacity to say yes to the journey no matter what Monkey Mind says. When you are willing, you become open and flexible. Flexibility is one of the most important traits you can possess as you begin your journey into the density, impermanence, and unpredictability of physical reality. If you become rigid about the way your game has to look, you will get discouraged at the border. Remember, one of the salient features of physical reality is that virtually *nothing* turns out exactly as you had planned. It usually turns out better (like my conference presentation), and it always provides you with lessons about mastery, which you will learn only if you are flexible.

Stage Two: Liftoff

During the second stage, liftoff, the high energy of metaphysical reality meets up with the swirl and natural density of physical reality. Think about the rocket ship, which burns most of its fuel at the beginning of its journey. For us, that fuel includes time, money, creativity, physical vitality, enjoyment (in the form of appreciation and staying present), and relationship.

At liftoff we meet up with obstructions to our best ideas about and splendid plans for how the journey was going to look. Unlike a rocket ship, which apparently powers its way through this stage, we learn at liftoff to *allow* what's going to emerge to do so. It's here that we observe and learn rather than control the voyage. In truth, that's what the rocket does as well; its sensors are always making minute corrections corresponding to the atmosphere, wind conditions, temperature, and so forth. Liftoff is never the straight shot that it appears to be to those of us on the ground looking up.

Normal obstacles are often deflating, frustrating events. Still, obstacles are a part of the hero's journey. If there were none, there would be no need to develop mastery. No obstacles, no growth. No growth, no hero's path.

The energy needed at liftoff, at the border between metaphysical and physical reality, is higher than at any other point on your journey. Whether it's launching a new product, directing a movie, opening a coffee house, starting to play tennis, or learning a language, the project almost always takes more energy — such as time, money, physical vitality — than we thought it would.

If that weren't enough, Monkey Mind always rises up at the border. It gives us very convincing reasons why we should stop, go back, or give up this new undertaking. Old synaptic pathways get activated, and we experience feelings of inadequacy or dread. For some, it's like we've become inexperienced kids again. Monkey Mind is devious, playing the tunes only we will dance to. Its voice is very compelling.

The following is a formula for bringing ease to your liftoff experience.

A. AT THE BORDER, SMALLER IS BETTER. Many of us want to race headlong into liftoff. We want to get the experience over with as quickly as possible, so we promise big results in order to truncate the experience. The trouble is, we end up like the proverbial bug on a windshield.

Let's try another analogy. People who jump into water from great heights do not die from drowning. On the contrary, if you are traveling fast as you hit the water, you don't go far at all. Past a certain point of speed, water can be as solid as concrete when you enter it — or try to. Yes, I know this is a graphic example, but we want to make a case for going slow at liftoff. Remember, even that rocket ship goes only a few feet in the first moments.

We'll take the water illustration a bit further. If you want to enter water with ease, do it a step at a time. Penetrating the surface at one mile per hour is obviously better than at eighty miles an hour. You will encounter a lot less natural resistance.

There is ease. If you take small steps instead of large dives at the beginning, your results may not be as dramatic, but you will actually get into the water more quickly.

Grant is an example of this principle. He was very successful at building his coaching business in a relatively short time period. I asked him to speak with some students at the coaching academy about how he did it. This is what he told them.

"When I first started my coaching business, I wanted to promise my own coach that I'd make twenty calls a day to prospective clients or others who might want me to make presentations about coaching to their organization. He insisted that I promise only five calls a day. He further invited me to make these five calls consistently every day for a month. I was to do nothing more or less than those five calls. That was my promise. I kept to it. It actually took more energy to do this than I thought it would."

That's exactly what happens during the liftoff phase of your game: you expend much more energy than you thought you would. Therefore it's a good strategy to go for small results at the beginning. Actually, the results may *seem* small, but they aren't, given the energy required to produce them. In fact, you could use this ratio: in the liftoff phase, you are putting in ten units of energy for every unit of results you achieve. And in some cases that is a conservative estimate. People who are successful in business know that projects can go over budget when the liftoff phase isn't taken into account. The bottom line is that it will almost always take more energy than you thought it would.

Robert Maurer, in his book *One Small Step Can Change Your Life*, reflects on the need for low-key changes.[1] The Japanese have a word for it: *kaizen*. The principle behind it is that small

consistent actions taken over time produce the most lasting results. It is a concept taken there by W. Edwards Deming, the quality improvement guru. Practicing *kaizen*, Japan was able to build
its post–World War II economy relatively quickly. People in organizations found small consistent ways to bring excellence and
efficiency to what they did. Soon businesses were booming.

On an individual level, this steadiness helps build new neu-
ral pathways in the brain. In addition, the small steps bypass
that part of our brain, the amygdala, that gets activated when
we want to make a departure from our usual safe routines. The
result: Monkey Mind has fewer reason to start screeching,
jumping up and down, and gesticulating wildly.

B. DO ONLY WHAT IS IN FRONT OF YOU. The urge to multitask
is strongest at liftoff. Because of the energy required at this
phase of your game, jumping over to another task can be
mighty tempting.

Monkey Mind may whisper that we could or should be
doing any number of things instead of what we are doing. It
might suggest we change to a new game worth playing. After
all, the excitement of metaphysical reality is preferable to the
mundane work of realizing a goal one step at a time.

Perhaps Elise's story will be all too familiar to you: "I
started to write a children's book on nutrition. The idea was
good. Then I hit the liftoff stage. I mistook the high energy re-
quirements for a sign that I shouldn't be writing that book. So
I decided instead to create a children's program on prosperity
for my church. But then things seemed to get too difficult, what
with the logistics of setting that program up and finding volun-
teers to help out. Another idea grabbed my attention: to create
a quilt project for children who had suffered the loss of a family

member. But then, you guessed it, I stopped and started thinking about yet another project. I seem to swing from idea to idea. I hit Stage Two and buckle."

The only way *through* liftoff is through liftoff. Remember that you are shaped by the game. The content of the game is not really important to your development as a hero on your path. What is essential is that you begin playing for something. This is how you discover who you truly are and the capacity you have for bringing clarity, focus, ease, and grace to your path. Elise could only experience success when she picked one of her ideas and saw it through.

C. PROMISE THE RESULT, NOT THE EFFORT. When we're at the border, it's tempting to promise, for example, how much time we'll spend at a given activity rather than promising what results that activity will produce. Let's look at Alex, who used these principles to build his own coaching practice.

"As I started building my coaching practice, I remember promising my own coach that I'd spend three hours each day calling prospective clients or looking for speaking engagements. She pointed out that I was promising the effort, in the form of time, rather than the results. That started me thinking about why, at the end of a busy day, I didn't experience any satisfaction. So I promised to contact three promising leads a day for individual, group, or organizational coaching. Something tangible in physical reality, no matter how small, gives me the sense that I'm working my way through those inevitable obstacles. In truth, some days it took me one hour to get in touch with three promising leads, and some days it took me four hours. The point was to promise that I would have something done by the end of the day."

A result is something concrete, something that you can measure. So, for example, developing a plan for reaching three people a day isn't really a measurable result. Making a list of who you're going to call is useful, but it's only the actual contact with another person that is the measurable outcome. There's the recipe for the cake, and then there's the actual baked cake (chocolate, please).

It's essential for your sense of satisfaction that you be able to point to something tangible that you have accomplished. It becomes a platform you can stand upon as you progress. Keeping your focus on results rather than effort brings you ease and saves you unnecessary frustration.

D. BRING WHO YOU ARE WITH YOU. Ontological conclusions are crucial at the border. They are powerful allies. They call out to your hero's heart and restore you to yourself. Monkey Mind's voice will always call to you, activating your natural inclination to doubt yourself or the game you created. However, once you shift the focus of your attention toward ontological conclusions, you begin to gather evidence for them, and you show up powerfully as the hero you already are.

You begin to focus on ontological conclusions the minute you ask yourself an ontological question. Here are some of those questions, brought forward from an earlier chapter with some minor modifications. When you aren't moving forward and Monkey Mind makes a pitch for giving up, focus for a moment on your answer to at least one of these ontological questions and experience a shift in your perspective.

- How might what I'm going through right now contribute to the lives of others?

- Where might I be driving in the fog?
- Where am I making this more difficult than it needs to be?
- What am I grateful for in this moment?
- Is it time to call someone who said they'd support me?
- What is emerging here?
- What lesson is here for me? How will it help me grow?
- What am I learning about my strengths and capabilities?
- How might I do the next thing before me with ease?
- Taking a look at one or more of your Standards of Integrity, ask yourself: How would someone who is courageous (wise, intelligent, creative, etc.) handle this situation?
- What am I *willing* to do next, whether I want to or not?

E. ACKNOWLEDGE EVEN THE SMALLEST RESULT AT THE BORDER. Finally, find something to acknowledge when you're at the border. You are at the nexus of creativity. This is where life is lived in vivid reds, yellows, greens, and blues. You are no longer sitting still with your dreams locked up in your head; you are applying energy to bring them to reality. Every step can be appreciated and savored.

When you acknowledge something, you are giving it life because you grant it existence. You are saying, "It is so." This may seem trivial, but it isn't. Many of us rush through our days producing results and discounting them because they weren't big enough. I see this all the time in seminars and private coaching sessions. Somehow we have a picture that success is equated with *quantity*, not *quality*. However, as we can see by now, the only way to luminosity is by doing what you promised to do with clarity, focus, ease, and grace.

Acknowledge the smallest results, and you bring those four qualities to bear upon your experience. You begin to see that your project lives or that your game is truly under way. Let me give you an example.

Jerry, a participant at a seminar I led over two evenings in southern Oregon, talked about having wanted for five years to write a mystery novel. He hadn't done anything about this, he explained, because he had writer's block. I didn't bother to ask him for his evidence for this writer's block because I knew he had five years' worth of it stored up. Instead, we had the following exchange:

Me: If you were to show up here tomorrow night having written one page of that book, would you be experiencing writer's block as you read us that page?

Jerry: But I have writer's block.

Me: Yes. However, if you were here reading a page to us tomorrow night, in that very moment would you be experiencing what you call writer's block?

Jerry: (Pausing) No, I wouldn't.

Me: So, the only thing that's standing between you and getting rid of this "writer's block" is one little page?

Jerry: I guess so, now that you put it that way.

Me: Are you willing to write one page and read it to us tomorrow?

Jerry: Yes, but it's so small. One page isn't a book.

Me: Are you willing to do it anyway?

Jerry: Yes, I am.

The next day he showed up at the seminar with one page. He read it to all eighty of us. It was about a dark Louisiana swamp and coming across an old crypt with initials on it and Spanish moss hanging down. Everyone was spellbound. They cheered for him, acknowledging his courage.

I asked Jerry if he experienced himself having writer's block that evening. You know the answer. In that moment he'd traded his reasons for his results.

I don't know if Jerry finished his book, but I do know that he was gutsy that evening in showing up for his dream. His story inspires me even today whenever I'm lured by my Monkey Mind into considering the possibility of giving up on writing.

In coaching people to write, I've sometimes had to whittle the promise down to one paragraph a day. Whatever it is, there's always something to acknowledge about a result at the border, even when it is small — especially when it is small!

Stage Three: Momentum

Imagine the rocket ship has broken free of the initial inertia of physical reality. Now it's going faster. The ratio of energy to results is more like one-to-one.

This is where you begin to breathe a sigh of relief because the game is starting to take shape. Here are some examples of how this phase might look:

- You are consistently walking those three miles each day to prepare for that twenty-mile hike along the Rogue River in Oregon.

- Your community speaking engagements regularly bring you at least one or two new coaching clients.

- You are putting away two hundred dollars a month toward your trip to Hawaii.

- Three pages a day on your novel? No problem!

You have successfully gone through Trouble at the Border. You are experiencing much more ease. You are fully engaged in the game. What's not to like?

Believe it or not, many people never make it past this point with their game. That's because the momentum phase is one in which your ability to focus energy is literally taken to the next level. Since you are producing results with more ease, there's the chance that you will begin to overpromise what you can do. There is a tendency to raise the bar too soon. Alex's story is illustrative here too.

"After I spoke at libraries and professional lunches and got a few interviews on local radio, the phone started ringing. Soon my business mushroomed to twenty clients weekly. I was pumped! But instead of staying there for a while and enjoying the fresh air of success, I raised the bar immediately. I started looking for ways to lead coaching groups over the phone. Now, don't get me wrong, phone coaching is great. It's just that I didn't give myself time to rest or savor where I was. I got very busy because now I had a new project — a phone group — and it was in liftoff. I could tell that I wasn't giving everyone my full attention. Then I got the flu. I think it was because I was working so hard."

The challenge during the momentum phase is to keep the promises you've made with clarity, focus, ease, and grace. You have put in a lot of energy during the liftoff phase. The results that you reap during this phase can give you a false sense of your capabilities and may mislead you into pushing the envelope too quickly. You'll only get exhausted doing that. Pace yourself for the rest of the game instead.

These are the points to remember in the momentum phase:

- Enjoy your results. Savor the sweetness of what you've produced!

- Continue to empower and inform your support team. Let them know if you're starting to bite off more than you can chew.

- If your project involves your professional growth, remember that people who are successful have developed the reputation of delivering consistently on their promises.

- Think twice about introducing a new project at this point. You may not want to be thrust into another liftoff just yet if it will affect your current game.

- Keep your Standards of Integrity close at hand. They will help you pace yourself. I'm not saying you must turn down new opportunities, just see to it that you maintain your focus on the present game as well.

Stage Four: Stability

The rocket ship has blasted off. It has gained momentum and is now in an orbiting pattern. Examples could look like this:

- You no longer have to call others to arrange speaking engagements; they are calling you.

- Your client base has grown to the point that referrals regularly make contact with you for appointments.

- The book manuscript is just about finished; only one chapter to go.

- You've taken such great care putting in that meditation garden that the plants are thriving and the fountain is gurgling.

- You have been keeping a regular training schedule, and only two weeks remain before your first half-marathon.

- There is a consistent flow of customers at your web-based gourmet chocolate cake business.

This is a time of great satisfaction and gratification. All that diligence and consistency have allowed your dream to blossom. But there's still more to learn about playing with ease.

Why? Because with stability comes entropy. Basically, entropy is the tendency of a system to lose energy over time, thereby gaining a measure of disorder. It's another way of looking at impermanence. While that rocket of ours is in orbit, a small amount of energy is lost through entropy. The amount can be very small. However, if no course correction is made, the rocket can eventually slow to the point where it no longer maintains its orbit.

Stability requires you to be vigilant about entropy. My own story is an example of this. When I first started my private psychotherapy practice, I would speak anywhere, anytime, about the benefits of having a therapist. When a prospective client would call, I would be on the phone within three hours to set up an appointment. I carried this quick-response pattern with me all the way through momentum. By that time, I was seeing twenty-five individuals and two groups each week.

Then something happened. I took my eye off the ball — not

good in most games! When a client called, I would wait twenty-four to forty-eight hours before getting back to them. By that time, some would have found another therapist. That didn't matter, I would say to myself, because more people would always call, as they had before.

This all went fine until one Monday morning when I looked at that week's calendar. I saw I had only twelve therapy hours, with no new clients on the horizon. The rocket had entered the atmosphere and was preparing to crash.

Any single lapse in focus doesn't mean much, but it can set up a pattern. A slow leak of energy ensues, and there you are, back at liftoff. I had to retrace my steps and start calling around to make further presentations and meet new people. In two months I was back where I had started before entropy, but this wasn't the most efficient, ease-filled use of my energy.

And, as ever, Monkey Mind is ready to start chattering, even in the stability phase. It tells you that it's okay to miss some days watering your new garden. It gives you great reasons to become complacent, to rest on your laurels for just a little while. That's the voice I was listening to as I let go of one new client after another.

The key points to bring ease to stability are:

- Look for energy leaks. Are you skimping on workouts, failing to return calls promptly, and so forth?

- Cut corners in what you're doing *only* if you can guarantee that it won't affect the quality of your game.

- This is the time to check up on the quality of your work. For example, if you lead seminars, make sure your material is up-to-date.

- Review your Life's Intentions and Standards of Integrity to make sure you're still on track.

It's during the stability phase of a project that we either reach our goal or find that we're back at liftoff. Here we run the race, paint the picture, create a thriving business, finish the screenplay — or start once again at the beginning. This is where we either say: "I did it!" or "Why didn't I do it?"

Follow the above guidelines, and the first alternative will be yours.

What comes after stability? A choice: either we can take the present game to the next level, or we can go on to other games worth playing and goals worth playing for. Even this delightful option can feel daunting. That's because we can get comfortable in the stability phase. We're experiencing a sense of mastery, but new levels of play or new games will put us face-to-face again with the unknown. Enter Monkey Mind. Letting go of how we've done things up until now may not *feel* good, but it is good. In fact, it can be a breakthrough.

Stage Five: Breakthrough

"Are you green and growing or ripe and rotting?" This quote from McDonald's Corporation founder Ray Kroc neatly sums up our need to continuously innovate and create our lives.

Janet, a bright, energetic business owner, has been looking forward to retirement. When she retired, which she hoped would be very soon, she'd go to college to complete her BA on the way to ministerial school. Trouble is that Janet's business needs her for at least two more years. Her plan is being thwarted, and she thinks this means her dream needs to be postponed.

Not necessarily. A breakthrough requires you to let go of the way you've been doing your life up until now. For Janet, this means revamping her neat, tidy finish-one-thing-then-go-on-to-the-next plan. It means calling the local state college to inquire about creative ways to achieve that BA while still working (such as enrolling in online courses). Janet needs to innovate and be creative with her dream, not defer it.

There's an old saying: "If it ain't broke, don't fix it." That's true in many situations. However, to experience breakthroughs, some kind of undoing is necessary. Keeping things the way they are, no matter how "unbroken," is not exciting. It doesn't stretch and invigorate you. Nor does it bring you closer to your dreams. This is not a formula for luminosity, is it?

To put you directly at the entry point to breakthrough, answer the following questions:

- Looking at my Life's Intentions, is there one that I dearly want to demonstrate but think that it's impossible given my current life?

- On a "Convince-O-Meter," with 10 meaning I'm really convinced and 1 indicating that I'm not so convinced, how persuaded am I right now that it would currently be impossible to do anything about this Life's Intention?

- Where might I need to let go of my conclusions and evidence about "how it has to look"?

- Am I willing to have a conversation with my supporters about creating a small, sweet goal that has to do with this Life's Intention?

- Am I willing to shift the focus of my attention from being comfortable to being revitalized?

When you begin to ask these questions, you put yourself outside your usual ways of seeing yourself. You look at yourself and your life with eyes that are clear and hopeful. Breakthrough is now possible.

That breakthrough is a new, or new and improved, game worth playing. Where do you go when you've gotten the idea for a game worth playing and goal worth playing for? Bingo. Back to the creation phase to begin once again. This cycle goes on throughout our lives; this is luminosity *in action*.

The density, impermanence, and unpredictability of physical reality — the very elements that make up a game — require us to be true to our Life's Intentions and goals but at the same time hold our plans lightly. If I hadn't learned that, I would never have climbed the stage that day at Hilton Head in my green sweats — and I probably would never have written this book.

CHAPTER ELEVEN

The Sum of Your Parts

Maintain coherence by bringing everyday actions into alignment with what is most important to you.

As a man's real power grows, and his knowledge widens, ever the way he can follow grows narrower, until at last he chooses nothing, but does only and wholly what he must do.

— Ursula K. LeGuin

The writer Ursula LeGuin says that people growing in power actually make fewer choices along their paths. How can this idea be uplifting? Don't we all want more choices, not fewer? I think LeGuin is speaking about how we become more sensitive to incoherence as we become more conscious and travel the hero's path. This chapter explores how, as your path grows more luminous, it also grows more compelling.

As you awaken to the presence of luminosity, you begin to automatically distinguish between those actions that lead you toward luminosity and those that lead away from it. The fog lifts, and you see which side of the road you're on. If necessary, you self-correct quickly, easily, and without a great deal of wasted energy. You have no choice, really, because you've *already* chosen the path of knowledge and power.

The following scenario describes what I'm getting at. Some version of it has happened to all of us.

You're walking down the street, minding your own business. You come upon a newspaper stand with its door open and newspapers inside. You bend down, take out a newspaper, and begin to walk on, intentionally not paying for it.

As you read this, your Monkey Mind might be jumping up and down saying, "I'd never do anything like *that*!" If that's the case, pick something you know you have done that is along the same lines.

To continue, as you move away from that newspaper stand, something remarkable happens. It's as though there were a big hand on the luminosity dial of your life, and it's turning luminosity down with each step you take. It's like a rheostat controlling your lightness of being. Colors, textures, and smells lose their vividness. At the same time, you begin to get tunnel vision because, like it or not, you can't stop thinking about what you've just done. In addition, less possibility and promise appear on the horizon. The sense that all is well fades away like the last golden rays of a sunset.

As that imaginary hand turns the luminosity dial down, Monkey Mind gets louder. As the light fades around you, Monkey Mind can be heard more and more clearly. It sounds something like this: "I deserve that paper for free today. After all, I work hard for my money, and I've paid for papers all my life. It's about time I get one for free. Besides, they don't print anything interesting nowadays, and those newspaper companies are just mega corporations who won't miss my money one bit.

Speaking of money, my boss hasn't even considered my promotion yet...and I heard a rumor that there would be no bonuses this year...and..."

You head for your office, your mind leaping from one Monkey Mind thought to another. None are particularly savory. All have a familiar ring. Given this starting point, you can fairly well predict what kind of a day you're going to have. That usual smile you have for your colleagues might not be there. The weekly staff meeting might start out on a sour note. You've begun to focus on the conclusion "I don't get what I deserve." Your brain is obliging you by gathering the appropriate evidence, and you're showing up as a reflection of it — frustrated, resigned, and maybe even cynical.

This inverse proportion law — that Monkey Mind grows in volume as luminosity fades — has far-reaching effects upon our daily lives. As we drift more and more off course, our generosity of spirit takes a backseat to our complaints. There is no mastery here — no clarity, focus, ease, or grace.

When Monkey Mind's chatter becomes strident and adamant — but not because you are encountering Trouble at the Border with a goal or project — chances are you're experiencing incoherence. This is best characterized as a state of discomfort that arises when we take action that is not in keeping with who we are in our hero's heart. Incoherence and ease are totally incompatible.

Getting back to the newspaper scenario, suppose you become more attuned to that luminosity dial and can notice changes more quickly. As you take that paper from the stand without paying for it, you instantly become aware of the darkness creeping in. It's even more noticeable because up until that

time you'd been experiencing a sense of goodwill and spaciousness. Because you notice Monkey Mind quickly, when it begins
its litany you know to ask, "What am I doing?"

Asking this question prompts you to go back, pay for your
paper, and close the stand's door. Immediately the big hand on
that dial of your life turns the luminosity back up to where it
was prior to the moment you took the newspaper. You go from
a state of incoherence to one of relief because the alarm bells are
no longer going off. Notice that it's always about taking action
— going from metaphysical to physical reality. For example, it
won't work to simply say to yourself, "I'll never do that again."
You must go back and do something to rectify the situation.

Coherence Is a Portal to Luminosity; Incoherence Slams the Door

According to the *Encarta Dictionary*, *coherence* means the "quality of being logically or aesthetically consistent, with all separate parts fitting together to form a harmonious or credible
whole." Synonyms for *coherence* include *lucidity* and *unity*. Lucidity relates to emitting light. It's all about luminosity.

Coherence is a principle we can employ that will point us
toward luminosity. It gives us a way to bring our everyday actions into alignment with what's important to us. It fosters our
personal well-being and helps us to be resilient during times of
complexity and change. It may already be obvious that coherence fosters the ease we're after.

This is how the coherence principle works. Whether we
know it or not, we have an internal guidance system made up
of the values that are important to us. If you've done the work

suggested earlier, you already have two clear indicators of what's meaningful to you: your Life's Intentions and Standards of Integrity. As we've seen, they live in metaphysical reality, and you bring them with you wherever you go. They are reflections of who you are ontologically — in your hero's heart — rather than psychologically. This makes them independent of your ever-changing thoughts and feelings. In this way they can become a potent internal guidance system that is not affected by the swirl of physical reality.

In physical reality, we are continually in action. Sometimes our action is focused, and sometimes it isn't. However, when this action produces an outcome that reflects our Life's Intentions or Standards of Integrity, we immediately experience harmony, meaning, satisfaction, and fulfillment. We experience coherence — and ease — because everything is coming together: who we are *inside* coincides with how we show up on the *outside*. Goodness is present, in the general sense of integrity or wholeness. In the moment of coherence, we see possibility and promise and know that all is well.

Let me show you what I mean. A few years ago it was about to be my Uncle Arnold's eightieth birthday. Aunt Gloria and I were talking about it as the three of us sat around the colorful table in her kitchen. The birthday was two months away, and she didn't think she'd be able to give Uncle Arnold the party he deserved because at age seventy-six, she was still following her life's passion by teaching second graders full-time, and her schedule was demanding.

One of my Life's Intentions is "To be a loving niece," so I got an idea: Would my aunt let me plan that party for Uncle Arnold? Her sigh of relief was my answer.

Two of my Standards of Integrity are "compassionate" and "creative." I asked myself how a compassionate and creative person would go about arranging this party. First, I interviewed my uncle to find out exactly what kind of party he wanted. If I was going to do something for someone else, it was important to be compassionate — in other words, to throw the birthday party he wanted, not the one I'd want for myself. Uncle Arnold is an earnest introvert. He wanted twenty to thirty of his friends to come to his home between 2:30 and 5:30 on the Saturday of his birthday. With Uncle Arnold's specifications in hand, I had a goal worth playing for.

His sons flew in from all over the country. The family worked together, and we prepared his favorite wine, his favorite foods — from brie cheese to beef skewers — and the most luscious, buttery cake you can imagine. Red roses and yellow ranunculus were smiling in blue vases. It was a sunny spring afternoon. At precisely 2:30 P.M. there came a knock on the front door. Uncle Arnold went to answer.

I was standing a few feet behind him. I could see him, the house we had decorated, and the dark oak door as he walked toward it. Opening the door, he saw four of his longtime friends, who chimed in unison, "Happy Birthday, Arnold!" My uncle did something I'd never seen him do before. He lifted his head back and gave a little laugh of pure delight.

At that moment I felt warmth around my heart, gratitude for being part of this event, and an instant recognition that life could not possibly get any better than this! It was coherence. It was luminosity. In that moment, who I am on the inside and what I had done on the outside coincided in a bouquet of harmony, meaning, satisfaction, and fulfillment. I was doing what I came here to do.

Now let's consider another scenario. In this case you still have Life's Intentions and Standards of Integrity, and you still take action. But here the action produces an outcome that somehow thwarts or goes against one of your intentions or standards. If you do nothing to rectify the situation, you start to experience frustration, resignation, and cynicism. These are symptoms of incoherence. I experienced a scenario like this, also with Uncle Arnold, that illustrates incoherence.

But before taking a look at it, let's look more closely at frustration, resignation, and cynicism. They are impediments to luminosity. They consume energy that could be used to forward our goals or to make the contributions that lie waiting in our hearts. They seem to follow in a sequence. That is, when incoherence is present, you first experience frustration. If you don't take action to correct the situation, frustration gives way to resignation. Finally, with prolonged incoherence, cynicism makes its appearance.

According to the *Encarta Dictionary*, frustration is "a feeling of disappointment, exasperation, or weariness caused by aims being thwarted." It's accompanied by aggravation, irritation, and annoyance — real energy wasters. People report that when they feel frustrated, their energy may be high but it's turned in on itself.

Resignation is linked to giving up, as in letting go of hope. When you resign from a project or goal, you quit and walk away from it. You become infused with evidence for why it won't work, either now or in the future. You begin to sound like Eeyore, the gloomy blue-gray donkey in *Winnie the Pooh*: "Don't bother. It won't work." When you are resigned, your energy is lower than in frustration: you've put a lid on it.

There's no creativity or chance for innovative thinking, which is what you really need at this point.

Cynicism is linked to pessimism, suspicion, distrust, scorn, and contempt. Whereas your energy is high when you're frustrated and low when you're resigned, with cynicism an icy quality is present. It's like the cold darkness of outer space, not a particularly beneficial environment for your heart. When cynicism is present, not only have you given up on an idea, dream, project, goal, or vision, but you are working against its possibility either now or in the future. You may begin to figure out how to make the project *not* happen.

I've seen cynicism on the faces of executives in boardrooms, nurses in hospital corridors, ministers at conferences, and therapists in seminars. We are all acquainted with its energy-sucking, steely quality. It should come as no secret that cynicism eliminates our options for luminosity.

Back now to the scenario I promised, again involving Uncle Arnold. It's definitely one that I'm not proud of, but it's a clear example of how things get mucked up and what to do about it.

About one year prior to his birthday party, we were at a family gathering in Atlanta. It was the night before a bar mitzvah, and about thirty of us were sitting in the reception suite of a hotel at about 11:00 P.M. I had just gotten in from California. I was talking with Uncle Arnold and three other family members about a business transaction I was about to complete. Uncle Arnold, who is an attorney and who has always looked out for me, voiced his concern about one of the conditions of the proposed contract.

In response, I heard myself say, "Uncle Arnold, I wish you'd stop treating me like a little kid!"

There was silence in that little group. All four of them looked at me. You know those moments when you just want to hide? This was one. I excused myself from the group, mumbling something about being tired, and made my way to my room.

With each step I took away from the reception suite, my heart felt heavier. At the same time, I heard Monkey Mind rationalize what I'd done. Feeling frustrated, I told myself that he didn't understand my affairs. Resignation came next, a weary "He'll never change the way he sees me." By the time I'd gotten to my room, it was clear: incoherence had set in.

I know my Life's Intentions and my Standards of Integrity. Nowhere does it say that I am willing "To be someone who yells at my Uncle Arnold." Not even close. I knew what I had to do.

The next morning, after a fitful night's sleep, I saw him and the three others at the restaurant in line for breakfast. I asked them all to join me. When we were seated, I turned to him and said, "Uncle Arnold, I want to apologize to you in front of everyone. What I said last night was rude and doesn't represent how much I love you and value your opinion. Please forgive me."

The relief I felt was mirrored on the face of each person at the table. Order was reestablished. The luminosity dial went back up to where it had been before my remark the night before. Of course Uncle Arnold said there was no need to apologize. He was generous, but I could see he appreciated it. We all had a great meal together.

It often doesn't take much to correct incoherence. The trouble is, we often wait so long that our hearts begin to fester. We get increasingly bitter as we slide from frustration to resignation and then to cynicism.

There is good news about incoherence. It is reflected in these words from Pema Chödrön: "There's a reason that you can learn from everything: you have basic wisdom, basic intelligence, and basic goodness."[1] If you did not have Standards of Integrity and Life's Intentions, it wouldn't matter to you if your actions did not reflect them. You would not care. The fact that you do care — that you experience frustration, resignation, and cynicism as the result of what you do — speaks to the golden nature of your hero's heart. There is no getting away from who you really are.

When we take corrective action, do things always turn out well? No, they don't. But consider this: what if you saw just a 50 percent improvement in your personal and professional life as you practice the principles for coherence?

You, Luminosity, and the Holographic Life

At the beginning of this chapter we talked about the effects of relatively small actions upon our entire experience of life in the moment. We saw how doing something as simple as taking a newspaper without paying for it can

- create the immediate experience of "endarkenment," in which we tune out from our physical surroundings, experience the onset of dread, and hear an increase in Monkey Mind chatter;

- encourage us to focus upon conclusions that are constricted, self-serving, and won't bring us anywhere near luminosity;

- set in motion a day that — to put it mildly — may not go as well as we'd like.

One way to appreciate how relatively small actions can produce such swift, far-reaching results is to consider the possibility that your life is holographic.

Everyone has seen holograms, whether in movies, as images on credit cards, or in art galleries. They're three-dimensional photographs made with the aid of a laser. These photographs have a special feature. If you take the holographic negative — or plate — of a tree, cut it into small pieces, and shine a laser through one of those pieces, you will still see the whole tree. That's because each part of a hologram contains information about the whole.

According to Michael Talbot in his exciting book *The Holographic Universe*, this "whole in every part" nature of a hologram provides us with an entirely new way of understanding organization and order.[2] And this means a new way of understanding the luminosity dial effect, or why a small action can influence our experience of our entire life in that moment. In other words, we don't have a work life, personal life, home life, and social life; we just have a life. Therefore, when we take action, no matter where we are or what we're doing, our *whole* life is affected in that moment.

Over thirty years ago David Bohm, a well-respected physicist, posited that we live in a holographic universe — that the universe has an underlying unity and indivisibility, and all things are infinitely connected in a seamless web.[3] He also suggested that we consider the holographic nature of our lives, whether it's looking at how we are interconnected with everything or considering that we can experience our individual lives holographically. Let's take this a bit further to see what it could mean for us.

Consider a second feature of holograms, one that helps explain how we truly experience our lives. It's called simultaneity. In a hologram, not only is every piece a part of the whole and you change the whole when you act upon one piece, but also the change is instantaneous. There is no linearity. Everything is connected nonlocally. That is, there is no space between parts of a hologram. In fact, Bohm suggested that the human mind creates the concepts of parts, space, and time in order to make sense of physical reality. From our perspective, it's useful to have those concepts if we're going to engage in games worth playing and goals worth playing for.

According to Talbot, in 1982 an extraordinary event took place at the University of Paris that supports this phenomenon of simultaneity.[4] A physicist there discovered that under certain circumstances subatomic particles such as electrons are able to instantly communicate with each other, regardless of the distance separating them. It doesn't matter whether they are ten feet or ten billion miles apart, somehow each particle always seems to "know" what the other is doing. It was as though they were not really separated by space at all but at some level were still intimately connected.

If we look at our lives as holograms, we see why we so immediately experience the result of our actions in coherence or incoherence. In fact, the more awake we are on this path toward luminosity, the quicker we see when luminosity is present and when it is absent. And we sense this shift in luminosity as relating to *everything* in our lives, not simply the particular act.

So far we've talked about unity and simultaneity. According to Bohm, these two features of the universe are joined by a third: the collapse of the past, present, and future as measurements of time.

How does this relate to luminosity? Well, think of it in terms of your life:

- Everyone wants to know how his or her life will turn out in the future.

- If we are living in a hologram where there is no real future in the linear sense, then how we are living life right now *is* our future.

- Therefore, if we want to know how our lives turned out, we look at how we are living them right now. We look at our everyday actions. *This* is how it all is turning out.

From one perspective, it is not comfortable to look at this. When, during seminars, I talk about this collapse of our future into our present, the group often holds its collective breath for a moment. We see our future extending before us full of promise; we want to believe that "the best is yet to be." Anyone suggesting that this glowing future is an illusion meets up with suspicion and dread.

Along with this dread comes the worry that we will never be able to effect change in our lives. Life makeovers, we think, take lots of energy in the form of time, money, and so forth. No matter how hard we try, there's too much to correct. So why even start?

But holographic principles give us hope — not in the future but in the now.

- If you wish to change your life, you only have to do something small. Because everything is interconnected, small actions lead to whole-life results.

- If you want to permeate your entire life with the fragrance of luminosity, simply practice doing the smallest thing in front of you with clarity, focus, ease, and grace. In the midst of a big undertaking, approach each incremental step this way, and each action will raise the luminosity quotient of every aspect of your life, simultaneously.

- Each step you take with clarity, focus, ease, and grace gives you your future, *now*.

The above provides us with additional incentive to look at Robert Maurer's book on *kaizen*, the art of making low-key changes.[5] Small, sweet steps, taken one at a time, not only change our life incrementally, they also instantly shift our whole life to a new level. Every time we take these steps with clarity, focus, ease, and grace, the hologram that is our life shifts in its entirety.

A famous Mother Teresa quote says this beautifully: "It is not how much we do, but how much love we put into the doing. And it is not how much we give, but how much love we put into the giving. To God, there is nothing small."

Getting to Coherence

Armed with a holographic perspective, we can now look at how to bring coherence to our lives on a consistent basis. Coherence creates the environment for luminosity. By now, it has to be abundantly clear that incoherence and luminosity can't exist together.

Method 1: Getting Relief

There's a difference between relief and joy. Relief is what you feel when you restore coherence to incoherent circumstances — going back and paying for your newspaper; apologizing to Uncle Arnold. We get relief by observing the things we do that cause us distress and then acting to restore coherence. Instead of pointing the finger at something outside us, we look at where our own action has produced outcomes that are not in keeping with our Standards of Integrity or our Life's Intentions. Here are some examples of incoherence:

- Promising to give a tithe to your church or source of spiritual nourishment and not doing it. This might be incoherent with the Life's Intention "To be a contributor to my community" or "To be spiritually developing."

- Forgetting to send a card or present to a friend, incoherent with the Life's Intention "To be a generous friend."

- Not paying your fair share of a restaurant bill when dining with a group of people, incoherent with Standards of Integrity such as "honest," "generous," or "friendly."

- Paying someone who works for you under the table, incoherent with the Life's Intention "To be financially successful."

- Taking something from the office, such as pads of paper and pens, incoherent with Standards of Integrity such as "trustworthy" and "honest."

- Gossiping about someone at the office, incoherent with the Life's Intention "To be a successful team player" or the Standard of Integrity "compassionate."

- Continuing to eat fatty foods after being told that your cholesterol level is high, incoherent with "To be physically fit and healthy."

- Cheating on your income tax, incoherent with "To be financially successful."

- Yelling at a member of your family, incoherent with "To be a loving family member."

- Leaving trash behind at a park or picnic area, incoherent with "To be a creator of beauty."

- Driving when you know you've had too much to drink, incoherent with Standards of Integrity such as "trustworthy" or "intelligent."

By now you're getting the idea: incoherence involves action that you have taken. What other people do or don't do is irrelevant here. We focus here upon exactly what we are doing that is making us miserable. Why? Because no matter how much we'd like to rationalize or put the Monkey Mind stamp of approval on it, incoherence saps energy and takes us away from our games worth playing and goals worth playing for.

The remedy for this kind of incoherence is simple. Whenever you experience frustration, resignation, or cynicism — however that occurs for you and whatever Monkey Mind symptoms come up — take out your Standards of Integrity and Life's Intentions. Look at them. Ask yourself the following:

- Which of these are staring back at me right now? If I were to pass an "Energy-O-Meter" over any of these Standards of Integrity or Life's Intentions, at what points would the needle register the energy of frustration, resignation, or cynicism?

- Am I willing right now to see where my own actions have produced outcomes that are not in keeping with the above?

- How would someone who has these Life's Intentions and these Standards of Integrity restore coherence?

- What is the first small, sweet action I am willing to take toward coherence?

Without waiting for frustration, resignation, or cynicism to arrive on the scene in full force, you may want to do the following. Look at your relationship with the six forms of energy — money, time, physical vitality, creativity, enjoyment, and relationship. Remembering the effective and ineffective use of each kind of energy, take a deep breath and do the following:

- Observe any ways in which you've acted incoherently with any of these energies. For example, are you spending lots of time playing computer games? Regarding physical vitality, have you been staying up too late at night with the result that you're too tired to exercise the next morning? Only you know where your incoherence lies.

- Are these actions producing outcomes that are not in keeping with some of your Standards of Integrity and Life's Intentions?

- If you see incoherence, look at how someone with your Standards of Integrity and Life's Intentions would clean up the situation.

- Given what you see above, promise to take one small, sweet step each day to bring coherence.

- Ask someone you love or admire to support you in taking this action. Allow yourself to receive that person's support.

Once you take this action, you get relief. The heart relaxes. You are at peace. You are stopping a drain on your energy.

Cleaning up incoherence is essential. However, doing this only brings us relief — a neutral state. Many of us get confused at this point. It's as though we think that when we get rid of a headache we have attained bliss. Getting relief only puts us on a good footing to actively create the experience of coherence. This is where we find satisfaction, meaning, harmony, and fulfillment. This is where luminosity resides.

Method 2: Actively Seeking Harmony, Meaning, Satisfaction, and Fulfillment

The second method is simple as well — an extension of what you practiced earlier as you were introduced to Standards of Integrity and Life's Intentions. It's proactive, and with it you can purposefully create your day. It works like this:

- In the morning, pull out your Standards of Integrity and your Life's Intentions.

- Pick one Life's Intention you're willing to deliberately demonstrate this day. (Start with one because more than one can get confusing.)

- In addition, pick two or three Standards of Integrity that you're willing to demonstrate this day.

- Write what you picked on a three-by-five card, and take it with you.

- Before each meeting, conversation, email, or phone call, pull out this card and ask yourself, "Am I willing to demonstrate this Life's Intention and these Standards of Integrity during this next interaction?"

- If your answer is yes — and by now we're assuming it will be — go ahead with what you're doing, occasionally bringing your focus back to this day's Life's Intention and Standards of Integrity.

- Notice if there has been a shift in how you show up or how the interaction went. In particular, you could use the diagram that follows to chart the results.

The Daily Practice of Coherence

Bonnie is a brilliant woman, full of ideas and creative methods. I was grateful when she showed me the evaluation tool she uses to keep track of clarity, focus, ease, and grace in everyday life. The basic idea for the following chart is hers, although I modified it somewhat to include coherence. The chart may support you in bringing these principles to life. You may wish to copy it onto a sheet of paper and then duplicate it.

EVERYDAY COHERENCE CHART					
Interaction or event:					
Life's Intention:					
Standards of Integrity:					
Degree to which each is present: 1 = very little; 5 = very much					
	1	2	3	4	5
Clarity					
Focus					
Ease					
Grace					

Guide

1. Interaction or event: What is the specific nature of the interaction? Are you meeting with a co-worker, talking on the phone with your mother, writing an email to a friend? If you're not interacting with other people, describe what you are doing, such as painting a picture, exercising, or cooking a meal.

2. Life's Intention and Standards of Integrity: Which Life's Intention and Standards of Integrity are you shooting for?

3. *Clarity* means being clear about who you are, what's important to you, the game worth playing. It also means being clear about who other people are in their heroes' hearts.

4. *Focus* means focusing your attention upon conclusions that are empowering, spacious, or ontological rather than

listening to Monkey Mind. Seeing people as the heroes they are is an example of this.

5. *Ease* means ease of action, whether at the border with a project or bringing it to completion. Ease happens when your actions in the moment are coherent.

6. *Grace* means being grateful for the journey, seeing that you are being guided by inner principles and that you can be resilient and centered no matter what is going on in physical reality.

7. Comments: Use this space to write down any details you notice. Is coherence present? Is this a luminous moment? What do you experience in your body or thoughts? Did something go better than expected? If it didn't, can you see a solution where you may not have seen one before?

I am asking you to measure clarity, focus, ease, and grace. I am not giving you a tool to measure luminosity. While these qualities are the critical elements of luminosity, luminosity is greater than the sum of its parts. If you are willing, it will surprise you with its appearance; it cannot be created with an expectation that it will look like a previous experience.

Use what you have read here in whole or part. Remember that it is small, sweet actions that are important here. You are shifting the hologram of your life if you look at even the smallest aspect of what we have just explored. That's because whatever you do with clarity, focus, ease, and grace immediately increases the luminosity in your life.

STEP FOUR

Cultivating Grace

CHAPTER TWELVE

The Spirituality of Luminosity

Honor your spirit by being willing and giving thanks.

We die on the day when our lives cease to be illumined by the steady radiance, renewed daily, of a wonder, the source of which is beyond reason.

— Dag Hammarskjöld

W hen I work with groups and we turn to the topic of grace, there's a subtle shift in the room. A feeling of hope arises and a sense that we are being guided by something bigger than ourselves. We could call it our voice of wisdom, intuition, or divine guidance. The name we give it doesn't matter. What does matter is that we sense the existence of something above and apart from physical reality that can shepherd us through its density, impermanence, and unpredictability.

We're going to look at the quality of grace from a number of different perspectives. First, the *Encarta Dictionary* defines it as "generosity of spirit." That's an ontological quality, making generosity of spirit one of the stepping-stones to luminosity.

A second definition is that grace is the infinite love, mercy, favor, and goodwill shown to humankind by God. In an interview with Michael Toms, Bishop John Shelby Spong reflected upon the nature of grace by explaining how the apostle Paul saw it: that we are loved by God no matter what we do.[1]

Yet another perspective on grace comes to us from essayist and philosopher William Hazlitt (1778–1830). He called grace "the outward expression of the inward harmony of the soul."[2] This is close to a definition of coherence — taking action that produces an outcome reflecting who we truly are. The experience of coherence is one of harmony, meaning, satisfaction, and fulfillment. As we've discussed, when we are living in coherence what's true on the inside is mirrored by actions taken on the outside.

In this chapter we'll use all three of these perspectives and look at how they pertain to our hero's journey toward luminosity. In truth, all three concern the same thing: how to use spiritual principles to wake up to the banquet of love and possibility that surrounds us so that our actions reflect our true nature and help us live the life we were meant to live.

I'm reminded of a conversation I had with a client. Cynthia and I are talking over the phone. It's a warm summer day, and I'm coaching her as she develops her own coaching business. She's taking small, sweet steps every day, and today she's grateful because a new client called after hearing her at the chamber of commerce mixer.

In the middle of our conversation, Cynthia recalls a recent dream. "In this dream I see a group of people sitting around a huge table. There's a feast going on, a real celebration. Some of these people are pushed back from this table with their eyes closed. Others are sitting closer to the table, but their eyes are still closed. Still others have their eyes open and are eating this most delicious food, in communion with everyone else. At this table, along with everyone else, are seated saints and wise people from all spiritual traditions. From time to time, a few sitting at the table with their eyes closed open their eyes, see that they're at a feast, and begin to enjoy their companions and savor their food. At that moment, a cheer goes up from the people around them, welcoming them to the feast."

Could it be that heaven is spread out before us right now like a banquet? Could it be that when we are hungry, it isn't because of an absence of spiritual food? How do we cultivate those moments Willa Cather described when "our eyes can see and our ears can hear what is there about us always"?

Let me pause a moment to clarify that by the word *spiritual*, I don't necessarily mean religious. Instead, I'm pointing to the timeless qualities we all possess that transcend our everyday thoughts, feelings, and concerns. In other words, we're looking at ourselves from that ontological, rather than psychological, viewpoint. A friend and mentor of mine, the Reverend Dr. Johnnie Colemon, once said, "You know how everyone is always saying that we are spiritual beings having a human experience? I say what's really happening is that we are *spiritual beings have a spiritual experience.*"[3] Amen!

Let me also clarify what I mean by *principle*. A principle is a guideline, an important underlying law or assumption required in a system of thought. It shows us the basic way in which something works. Spiritual principles are therefore basic underlying laws that show us how to wake ourselves up to our true nature, how to see and hear it. We find such principles in countless wisdom traditions because they are universal. Let's take the twelve steps of Alcoholics Anonymous, for example. Although they're based upon the Oxford Group's exploration of early Christianity, these steps are nevertheless spiritual principles that millions of people have used successfully, whether or not they have a religious affiliation.

Spiritual Principle: It Works if You Work It... but *How* Do You Work It?

The Reverend Dr. Johnnie Colemon has also been known to say, "It works if you work it," a catchy phrase that has found its way into twelve-step and spiritual groups around the world. I like this emphasis on action. We may very well benefit from meditating on our spiritual principles, but we're on the path to luminosity when we live them, act upon them, "walk our talk." How do we know when we're using spiritual principles in the way they're meant to be used? How can you tell you're on the right track?

People who are successful do what's meaningful to them with clarity, focus, ease, and grace. Many of them have learned how to use spiritual principles in powerful ways. You will too when you add the following to your luminosity tool kit.

BRING YOUR CAPACITY TO BE WILLING WHEREVER YOU GO. We began this book by talking about being willing. It is one of the most powerful spiritual principles you can use. It's spiritual because it puts you in touch with your capacity to transcend your doubts, worries, and preoccupations. It is your ability to say yes to everything on your hero's path.

David is a body worker in Omaha. He comes with a ready

smile and a faint odor of lavender permeating his skin after hours of massage. He talks to me about how being willing has helped him. "Being willing has helped me become spiritually supple. By that, I mean I'm not so attached to having things turn out exactly as I envision them. I don't clench up. When I started this massage business, I was willing to have other people support me as I looked for an office. I asked for advice and actually took it more often than not. I didn't give my usual 'yes, but' to what they offered. As a result, everyone became my guardian angel."

When you're supple, you're limber and elastic. You can bend with the swirling energy in physical reality. You respond more quickly to the changing landscapes that emerge unpredictably because you are not rigidly bound by a specific course of action. You say yes and dance with whatever comes before you.

BEFORE YOU USE A SPIRITUAL PRINCIPLE, MAKE SURE IT'S A PRINCIPLE AND NOT A RULE. Both rules and principles are important. It's obvious that you need to know the rules of a game worth playing before you can begin to play it successfully. But that's not what we're talking about here. This is a more subtle distinction, the ignorance of which causes mischief in our lives. It all begins with Monkey Mind.

Monkey Mind has the emotional, mental, and moral development of a nine- to eleven-year-old. One feature of that level of thinking is that it is very concrete. Have you ever tried to talk with a child about the "principle" behind something the child was doing? That blank look you got wasn't resistance, it was incomprehension; the child didn't know what you were talking about.

For example, the reason a nine-year-old won't steal something, *really*, is because he or she could get into trouble, not because of an underlying principle of, say, coherence and incoherence.

Fast-forward to our own lives. If you take a spiritual principle and run it through your Monkey Mind grid, it turns into a rule. Instead of helping you reach into your heart to bring forth your contribution, this rule is now a source of frustration and possibly dread. Let me show you what I mean.

People naturally want their lives to contribute to others. Veteran fund-raiser and global activist Lynne Twist, in her book *The Soul of Money*, refers time and again to our basic desire to share what we have in order to make a difference in the lives of others.[4] Her book is filled with stories of people who have courageously gone out of their way in order to do this.

In spiritual communities, there is a natural desire to give back to the source of our spiritual nourishment. It's called tithing. It is meant to be a foundation for personal empowerment. However, empowerment is not always what happens when this spiritual principle is interpreted by Monkey Mind.

One way to look at the spiritual principle behind tithing is to see that it provides us with the opportunity to demonstrate compassion, generosity of spirit, and gratitude. In short, we get to show up as who we truly are in our heroes' hearts. Seen in this way, the reward we receive when we tithe is instantaneous. It is the capacity to tithe itself, the opportunity to demonstrate our ontological nature. As we give back to the source that has nourished us, our eyes open to the banquet of luminosity that has been waiting for us all along. We eat at the table with our teachers.

But tithing takes on different characteristics in the hands of Monkey Mind. First is the notion that if I give money, I should get something in the future in return — more money, a new relationship, or an expanded business opportunity, for instance.

Giving with the expectation of receiving in the future is not practicing a principle; it's bargaining, quid pro quo. You can't use a principle to negotiate this kind of deal. In fact, spiritual principles do not concern themselves with the future, since in the domain of metaphysical reality, linear time is an illusion. When we focus on what we want to get later, we don't see how our lives could shift holographically, *right now*. We are focused on future rewards instead of seeing the treasure we were given the moment we contributed.

If you remember our earlier discussion of conclusions and evidence gathering, giving with the expectation of later receiving leads us to the conclusion "the best is yet to be." As we wait — tap our fingers, grow impatient, and perhaps become frustrated, resigned, and cynical — we don't see that the best is right now. And right now. And right now.

Taking this idea a step further, according to Monkey Mind, something dreadful will happen to us if we *don't* tithe. We'll "draw" negative consequences toward us and never have the opportunities we seek. But spiritual principles aren't about what's good or bad, positive or negative. Those are *psychological* judgments, which don't occur in the same domain as spiritual principles. What happens when you don't tithe? You simply spend a little more time at that table with your eyes closed.

So this is the difference between a spiritual principle and a rule:

- A rule is something that you sense is being imposed upon you from without. If you don't follow it, something bad

will happen. It is certainly true in some domains —
when you're driving, for example. But we all have this
underlying reaction to rules: they're made to be broken, or at least gotten around.

- A spiritual principle comes from within. You hear your
  voice of wisdom, not your Monkey Mind. When you
  heed it, you wake up. You experience grace, a sense that
  all is well, and maybe an opening for possibility. Your
  body relaxes. When you don't follow a spiritual principle, there's a flatness. It's not that you are punished,
  it's more like neutrality: nothing lost or gained.

Want to know when you're listening to Monkey Mind and
when you're in the presence of a spiritual principle? If your
body is tight around the heart or solar plexus, if you feel dread
or fear, or if you are thinking about right or wrong, good or
bad, chances are it's Monkey Mind talking. If you experience instead an expansive quality, the fog lifting so that you see things
more clearly than before — as well as a possibility for action —
then it's a spiritual principle.

LEARN TO PRACTICE SPIRITUAL PRINCIPLES PRECISELY. There
is a scene in one of the popular Harry Potter movies. All the
young wizards are sitting at a long table, learning how to
cast a levitation spell. As they flick their wands, nothing happens. Then Hermione pronounces the incantation precisely
— "Wingardium Leviosa" (win-GAR-dee-um lev-ee-OH-sa) —
and produces the desired effect.

I've learned from people who practice spiritual principles in
their daily lives that if you want to receive the benefit for which
a principle was designed, you must practice it precisely in the

way it was given. This is often not as simple as it sounds. I don't know about you, but my own Monkey Mind can come up with great embellishments, trimmings, and flourishes to tried-and-true spiritual principles.

My friend Paul echoed this best in what he confided to me as we sat waiting for a plane one evening in the Denver airport: "As you know, I'm in the twelve-step program of Alcoholics Anonymous. I have a sponsor, who's the most patient person in the world, a true saint, if you ask me. When I started the program three years ago, I'd get into these big arguments with him about why Step 2 should really be Step 3. Actually, he wouldn't really argue with me at all. He'd sit back over his pancake breakfast and give me this wide smile. I remember one day he said to me with a chuckle in his voice, 'I suppose you're gonna want to redesign the whole Step 3 process next, aren't you?' Only later did I see that I hadn't had the faintest idea about how to practice spiritual principles. Now I do: be precise and don't put in my own two cents' worth."

This emphasis on precision is not part of a cosmic conspiracy to trip us up. It's actually a way to silence the "but what about this?" and "shouldn't we also..." of Monkey Mind. Precision simplifies; Monkey Mind makes things more difficult than they need to be.

Precision is also practical. Earlier in the book I made a case for using the words *being willing* rather than *willingness* when you want to lift the fog from your hero's path. Over the years, a few people asked if that was being too nitpicky. I don't blame them. I thought it was myself until I noticed that one word, *willing*, produced the desired effect and the other, *willingness*, didn't.

Or take another example. You've now been given a number of ontological tools: your Standards of Integrity, Life's Intentions, a list of ontological questions, and ways to see other people as they are meant to be seen. All of these tools provide you with anchors for dealing with the complexity of physical reality. If you practice with them in the way that's suggested, I guarantee you'll experience clarity, focus, ease, and grace in virtually every area of your life. And sooner than you think!

TAKE PRINCIPLED ACTION. You can only claim to have mastered a spiritual principle if you are demonstrating it consistently in your everyday life. People we admire encourage us to take what we know in metaphysical reality and put it into physical reality. Mother Teresa's motto was "love in action." We've heard "treat, and move your feet." From the book of James we learn that "faith without works is dead." By universal consensus, the only way we can claim mastery is by demonstrating it, not by intellectual knowledge or willpower alone.

Especially not by willpower alone. It's appealing to believe that if we were to direct our thoughts strongly enough in the direction of our ideas, the results we desire would be drawn to us like a magnet. As a result, we might spend time visualizing our dreams without taking any action to go out and attain them. However, visualization without action, just like an intention without action, is really just a recipe for frustration, resignation, and cynicism.

The ontological realm is not the Land of Magical Thinking — or Hermione's spells. Luminosity is the result of focused *action*. We focus our attention on conclusions that matter to us, and our *behavior* naturally aligns, coheres. We keep our eye on our Life's Intentions, Standards of Integrity, and the hero in others, and we *act* accordingly. We ask the right questions about who and where we are, and the fog lifts so that we can *move* into the proper lane and avoid becoming spiritual roadkill.

We become spiritual roadkill when we passively apply spiritual principles (actually an oxymoron). For instance, countless times over the years I've been asked, "How can I manifest more money in my life?" I answer, "You mean other than by earning it, saving it, investing it wisely, and not leaking it? Other than that?" You must take action. As we've seen, being financially successful can be a Life's Intention. It is doing what you said you'd do — with money — with clarity, focus, ease, and grace. It can be the impetus for a rewarding game worth playing. This is not a passive process. The idea is realized in physical reality, which is the domain of action and visible results.

But just any old action won't do. Just as faith without works is dead, work without faith is exhausting. That's when we become driven. It's when our lives take on the quality of one to-do list after another. The meaningful life is not exhausting at all. It may not be easy, but it is suffused with ease. It is also simple to achieve. Just make sure that the actions you take in physical reality are informed by the principles you've been given here, and you're home free.

SHIFT THE FOCUS OF YOUR ATTENTION FROM RESPONSIBILITY TO PRIVILEGE. A number of years ago I heard the following story from a participant during a seminar I led at Esalen Institute in California. We were standing on a grassy cliff overlooking the calm Pacific. The sunset was extraordinary: fiery orange clouds below and just the beginning of stars in a royal blue sky above. It was the perfect backdrop for what Phil told me.

"My dad died last year. We were lucky because he was lucid

up until the end, and not in much pain. We took him home from the hospital so that he could make his transition in familiar surroundings. One afternoon I was there reading some poetry to him. He said to me, 'Phil, it's funny how things look different to me. The things I complained about in the past or that I thought were such heavy responsibilities — all those things seem like privileges right now. Even stuff like taking out the garbage or paying income tax. I saw them as big responsibilities and burdens. I wish I had seen them as privileges instead.'

"My dad passed away about one month later. But his words have stuck with me all this time. Whenever I start to grumble about what I have to do, I cut it out fast, and you know what? It really *was* a privilege to take my eight-year-old son to the dentist last week!"

In chapter 7 we looked at the Four-Box Model, which showed how we create our personal paradigms. We saw that our brains are constantly forming conclusions about everything, whether we're aware of it or not. We also learned that once we focus on one of these conclusions, the brain begins to gather evidence to support it. If you are focused on the conclusion known as "responsibility," you're going to gather evidence for how much of it you have. That synaptic trail will become well worn.

We further discovered that we show up as the immediate reflection of the evidence we're currently focused upon. Our behavior, both verbal and nonverbal, is automatic.

It doesn't take much imagination to see how life unfolds for us when holding the conclusion "I have responsibilities." We're yoked to a heavy load. There's not much enjoyment, let alone breathing room. We can become sourpusses before we know it. Synonyms for *responsibility* are *job*, *duty*, *task*, and *blame*. Synonyms for *privilege* include *freedom*, *opportunity*, and *benefit*. Which do you choose?

Try using *privilege* in the place of *responsibility* for thirty days. Keep track of any shift in your relationships with loved ones, colleagues, or friends. Observe how you show up in your life and how others react. I wager you will note an opening for possibility, relationship, and enjoyment. You will have more energy.

DON'T SETTLE FOR HAPPINESS. Spiritual principles put us in the domain of luminosity, not happiness. Remember my childhood examples from my mother's bakery? Plunging my arm into a vat of chocolate was a happy moment. Saving money from my work in the bakery and buying a meaningful Mother's Day gift was a luminous moment.

Having read this far, you know I have nothing against happiness. (And you've surely noticed I have nothing against chocolate!) But when we settle for happiness — or when we make it our goal — we remain in the psychological realm of thoughts and feelings. We're at the mercy of the constantly shifting weather there (not to mention the smog and fog). We can do better.

CONSIDER YOUR CONTRIBUTION. Speaking of doing better, I'd like to make explicit now something that has been implicit in our exploration of the luminous life. Luminosity is ultimately about discovering ways to contribute something to others. In this way, the hero's journey is really a spiritual journey.

Joseph Campbell said that the ultimate stage for a hero is when he or she brings back from the journey gifts that will benefit the community. Other traditions teach the same idea. In

the twelve-step tradition, service is the principle behind Step
12. The St. Francis prayer is about becoming an instrument for
the benefit of others. The spiritual path is about going inward
to find what's important to you but then also going outward to
do something in physical reality that will benefit not only your
life but also the lives of others.

Even solitary pursuits can be a contribution. That's because
we are all connected in a web of relationship. Everyone is inspired by those who follow their dream. We've seen the lives of
a wife and child enriched by a father's picture-painting goal.
We've explored how asking others to support you actually
gives them the chance to make a difference. The knowledge
that their presence counts for something is, after all, what people
want most in their heart of hearts.

I've described how shifting my attention away from my
sloppy sweats and disheveled hair and onto how I could make
a contribution to my listeners turned a potentially disastrous
speech into a success instead. Take a moment to reflect for yourself on how your own dreams, games, and goals have encouraged others on their hero's journey. Your actions will gain even
more meaning for you when you do.

CULTIVATE GRATITUDE, THE KEY TO GRACE. A while ago I
was fortunate to visit Mile Hi Church in Colorado, where
I heard Dr. Roger Teel, senior minister, talk about a woman
who, although blind and ill, nevertheless considered herself to
be the "richest woman in the world." The story is inspirational.
There she is, living in a small trailer, unable to leave and visit
her friends. Her husband has passed away. By all outward ap-
pearances, she should be sad and depressed. And yet people are

happy to come to visit her and take care of her. They want to be around her, with her infectious smile and gentle laugh. She's clearly gathering evidence for everything for which she is grateful.

People have dealt powerfully with disease and dismal circumstances by lifting their minds and opening their hearts to the gifts that surround them. Through gratitude we automatically place ourselves on the path to luminosity.

Paradoxical as it may seem, the spiritual principle of gratitude has little to do with our physical surroundings and everything to do with becoming "spiritually supple." To be grateful is to be openhearted and vulnerable.

Did I say vulnerable? You bet I did. There's a way to look at this that won't frighten you or arouse Monkey Mind. From a spiritual perspective, to be vulnerable is to allow the winds of life to blow freely over your heart. It means to be permeable — to let life in. Sounds a lot like being willing, doesn't it?

When I look into the eyes of people I consider to be mentors, teachers, or guides, I find something very interesting: they are vulnerable and defenseless. I've seen this while looking at photos of Mahatma Gandhi, Martin Luther King Jr., Mother Teresa, Paramahansa Yogananda, Myrtle Fillmore, and Eleanor Roosevelt. By *vulnerable*, I mean, once again, that they're letting life in on its own terms. By *defenseless*, I mean the following: when you see that you have nothing to defend, you can stop putting energy into being defensive.

Think of all the energy we'd save if we didn't use it to defend ourselves, if we realized once and for all that there's nothing that needs defending. Think about how you might put that energy to better use. Gratitude is easiest when we are willing to become vulnerable and defenseless.

Monkey Mind rails against gratitude. It tells us that we'd better be careful not to relax our vigilance or something very scary might happen and we won't be prepared.

So to develop gratitude, begin with small, sweet steps, the *kaizen* of gratitude:

- Every evening, make a list of three things for which you are grateful. Keep this in a notebook that you place by your bed. They could be incidents that occurred during the day, such as a beautiful sunset, letter from a friend, or an unexpected check in the mail. Or they could have to do with realizing something great about your children, husband, wife, or partner.

- Just make sure that you take a few moments to get in touch with what, specifically, you are grateful for. Let the texture of it get next to your skin. It's more important to truly savor one instance of gratitude than to list forty of them in an offhand way.

- If you hear Monkey Mind say, "I can't think of anything to be grateful for today," tell it, "Duly noted," and nevertheless shift your attention to three things for which you are grateful.

This brief, simple act trains you to gather evidence for gratitude. As you may recall, as you do this you are creating new synaptic pathways. You are literally restructuring your brain to look for evidence of what is working in your life as well as what is important to you. This is a subtle yet powerful reorientation. Work it and see how it works!

Where the Luminosity Path Has Led Us

We have not even to risk the adventure alone, for the heroes of all time have gone before us. The labyrinth is thoroughly known. We have only to follow the thread of the hero's path, and where we had thought to find an abomination we shall find a god. And where we had thought to slay another, we shall slay ourselves. Where we had thought to travel outward, we shall come to the center of our own existence. And where we had thought to be alone, we shall be with all the world.

— Joseph Campbell, *The Hero with a Thousand Faces*

It's time for us to complete this part of your journey. Before we do, let's take a moment and review where we've been.

We began by looking at what luminosity is all about. It's a sense of possibility and promise, a sense that all is well and that we have everything we need to be successful on our hero's journey. In luminous moments we're not regretting the past or worrying about the future. We're simply grateful to be where we are, right here and now.

We saw that luminous moments aren't the same as happy ones. The essential difference is that during luminous moments we're engaged in a game worth playing and goals worth playing for. That quality of engagement keeps us vital and supple, ready to take what's in our hearts and bring it into the density, impermanence, and unpredictability of physical reality. Luminous moments bring meaning and purpose to life. We saw that we can grow way beyond where we have stopped ourselves in the past and that we are shaped simply by engaging in those games that are important to us.

We discovered aspects of who we are that transcend our

doubts, worries, and judgments: our Life's Intentions and Standards of Integrity. These are ontological qualities because they point to a way of being rather than ways of thinking and feeling. They serve as the guideposts toward luminosity. Like the shepherd's rod and staff, they keep us on the path. When we experience the incoherence of frustration, resignation, and cynicism, we know we've temporarily strayed from the path — but we've learned how to get back to ourselves in order to move on.

We saw the nature of the playing field. There is metaphysical reality, the home of ideas, dreams, vision, and meaning. There is physical reality, where we show up for the game. There are goals that matter. And there is Trouble at the Border. We saw that mastery requires obstacles, that without them mastery is meaningless. Hence the border experience is important to the development of our skill as well as our spirit.

At the border we met Monkey Mind, that aspect of the mind that chatters at us. It's the normal outgrowth of our need to survive during prehistoric times by looking at everything that could go wrong in any situation. That's why it urges us to quit the journey altogether or at least wait until we are comfortable. But we saw that the luminous life is not necessarily the comfortable life and that we can lean into discomfort as we make our way toward our goals.

Along the way we saw some practices for learning to observe our lives, to gain some elevation above the smog of our usual thoughts, and to see others for who they really are. This gives us breathing room to shift the focus of our attention to conclusions that matter instead of holding conclusions that lead far from luminosity. We learned that our brain constantly gathers evidence to support the conclusions it brings to everyday life and that the brain is more malleable than we thought.

We discovered a surprise: our incoherence — the frustration, resignation, and cynicism we experience when our actions produce outcomes that don't reflect who we are — is a reflection of our basic goodness. If we didn't have Life's Intentions and Standards of Integrity, there'd be no incoherence, no matter what we did.

We learned how to bring ease to our game, how to take small, sweet steps that bypass Monkey Mind, and how to focus our energies at each stage along the way so that our goals and dreams come alive with possibility and promise.

The labyrinth is thoroughly known. May you embrace your heroic journey, saying yes to your dreams and thank you to life. It has been my privilege to be with you here, on the path to luminosity.

Acknowledgments

It is possible to create a book only with the support of others. There are many people who have made a difference to this work and to me personally.

First, it is with gratitude that I acknowledge all the teachers of my life from many spiritual and wisdom traditions. Although they are too numerous to mention here, I want to give special acknowledgement to those whom I drew from for this book: Joseph Campbell, who wrote that our hero's path is thoroughly known and that we have only to begin it; Paramahansa Yogananda; Rev. Dr. Johnnie Colemon; Sogyal Rinpoche; Pema Chödrön; and others mentioned or quoted in the text of the book. I give them all thanks for pointing the way.

Thousands of participants in the Academy's courses, including the Mastering Life's Energies course, have helped me to clarify the principles you will find here. They have been and continue to be a courageous source of inspiration for me.

I have also come to appreciate at a deeper level those in the publishing world who support this work: Kim Witherspoon and Alexis Hurley of Inkwell management have continued to encourage me to write; Marc Allen, who grasped the opportunity immediately; editors — Georgia Hughes, Yvette Bozzini, Kristen Cashman, and Priscilla Stuckey — who took the manuscript and made it shine.

Holding my feet to the fire while lovingly supporting me was my coach, Sally Cooney Anderson. Lending to the refinement of the principles and the vision of expansion of the efforts that brought the book to this stage were the Academy for Coaching Excellence staff and community: Beth Ann Suggs, Wayne Manning, Nicolette Bautista, Sally Babcock, Margi Mainquist, Carole Rhebock, Ward Peters, Carolyn Ingram, Patrick Davis, Ann Schumacher, John Harrison, John Smith, Chuck Iverson, Michele Vesely, Tina Weinmeister, Susan Gnesa, Nancy DeCandia, Sheree Keely, Erick Hill, Lilly Stoller, Julie Stanek, Kris Wiley, Karen Grigsby, Mary Tumpkin, Diane Philpot, Harry Morgan Moses, David Thomas, Marti Bolton, Julie Bowden, and Linda Rusch. And, in memoriam, to those who loved this work but are no longer with us, Ally Milder and Donna Westmoreland. I could actually make another book of acknowledgments, so I hope those not named understand that at this age my heart is fuller than my memory cells.

Family lives through all the ups and downs of the author and gives unconditional support: Rita Saenz; Gloria and Arnold Stone; Lisa, Chuck, Rachael, and Bea Simon; Toni and Jerry Yaffe; Susan and Andrea Saenz, the other family authors; and Dan Pawson, Andrea's husband. I love and appreciate you all.

Notes

Introduction

1. Willa Cather, *Death Comes for the Archbishop* (1927; New York: Vintage Classics, 1990), 50.

Chapter 1. Being Luminous

1. Maria Nemeth, *The Energy of Money: A Spiritual Guide to Financial and Personal Fulfillment* (New York: Ballantine Wellspring, 1997).
2. Joseph Campbell and Bill Moyers, *The Power of Myth* (New York: Doubleday, 1988; reprint: Anchor, 1991), 186.
3. Campbell and Moyers, *The Power of Myth*, 283–84.

Chapter 3. A Game Worth Playing

1. Thich Nhat Hanh, *Essential Writings* (Maryknoll, NY: Orbis Books, 2001), 19–20.
2. Sogyal Rinpoche, *The Tibetan Book of Living and Dying* (San Francisco: HarperSanFrancisco, 2002; reprint, 2004).

Chapter 6. Your Standards of Integrity

1. See, for example, Martin Heidegger, *Ontology: The Hermeneutics of Facticity* (Bloomington, IN: Indiana University Press, 1999).

Chapter 7. Draw Your Own Conclusions

1. Malcolm Gladwell, *Blink: The Power of Thinking Without Thinking* (New York: Little, Brown, 2005).
2. Gladwell, *Blink*, 23.

Chapter 8. What Are You Looking At?

1. Ram Dass, in an early interview with Michael Toms, available at http://www.newdimensions.org.
2. Mother Teresa quoted in Wayne Teasdale, *The Mystic Heart* (Novato, CA: New World Library, 2001), 109.

Chapter 9. Energy Efficiency

1. Joseph Campbell, *The Power of Myth* (1988; New York: Anchor, 1991), 19.

Chapter 10. It's How You Play the Game

1. Robert Maurer, *One Small Step Can Change Your Life: The Kaizen Way* (New York: Workman, 2004).

Chapter 11. The Sum of Your Parts

1. Pema Chödrön, *Start Where You Are: A Guide to Compassionate Living* (Boston: Shambhala, 2004), 78.
2. Michael Talbot, *The Holographic Universe* (New York: Harper, 1991; reprint, 1992), 20.
3. David Bohm, "The Enfolding-Unfolding Universe and Consciousness," in *The Essential David Bohm*, ed. Lee Nichol (New York: Routledge, 2003), 97.
4. Talbot, *The Holographic Universe*, 52.
5. Robert Maurer, *One Small Step Can Change Your Life: The Kaizen Way* (New York: Workman, 2004).

Chapter 12. The Spirituality of Luminosity

1. Michael Toms with John Shelby Spong, Radical Reformation and a New Renaissance, audio program available at http://www.newdimensions.org, programs 2798 and 3098.
2. William Hazlitt, "On Manner," available at http://en.wikiquote.org/wiki/William_Hazlitt.
3. Johnnie Colemon said this to me in person, but her book *Open Your Mind and Be Healed* (Los Angeles: DeVorss, 2000) presents her teachings in detail.
4. Lynne Twist, *The Soul of Money: Transforming Your Relationship with Money and Life* (New York: Norton, 2003).

Index

About the Author

Maria Nemeth, PhD, MCC, is a licensed clinical psychologist and master certified coach. In 2002 she founded the Academy for Coaching Excellence to make coaching principles more widely available. Maria has thirty years of experience in the design and delivery of transformational training programs to corporations, healthcare institutions, professional associations, ministries, and nonprofit organizations. She has served as assistant professor in clinical psychology at California State University Dominguez Hills and as associate clinical professor in the department of psychiatry at University of California Davis School of Medicine.

Maria's previous book, *The Energy of Money: A Spiritual Guide to Financial and Personal Fulfillment*, was published by Ballantine Wellspring in 1999 and is available in five languages. Her nine-hour audio series, *The Energy of Money*, won the 1999 Audie Award for Best Personal Development Series. She lives in Sacramento, California.

To learn more about her work or to contact Maria Nemeth about a workshop, go to the Academy's website at: www.academyforcoachingexcellence.com.